William Forbes

Memoirs of a Banking-House

William Forbes

Memoirs of a Banking-House

ISBN/EAN: 9783337117672

Printed in Europe, USA, Canada, Australia, Japan

Cover: Foto ©ninafisch / pixelio.de

More available books at **www.hansebooks.com**

MEMOIRS

OF A

BANKING-HOUSE

BY THE LATE
SIR WILLIAM FORBES OF PITSLIGO, BART.
AUTHOR OF THE 'LIFE OF DR BEATTIE.'

SECOND EDITION.

WILLIAM AND ROBERT CHAMBERS,
LONDON AND EDINBURGH.
1860.

Edinburgh:
Printed by W. and R. Chambers.

INTRODUCTORY NOTICE.

THE public is here presented with a Memoir, the genuine composition of Sir William Forbes, regarding the history of a mercantile establishment, of which he was long the chief. The manuscript having been accidentally shewn to the editor, he saw in it so much that was interesting, as to be induced to plead with Sir William's surviving friends for permission to place it before the world. It is consequently published at the distance of fully fifty-six years from the time when it was written, for the author appears to have closed his narration in May 1803.

The private banking-house so long known in Scotland in connection with the name of Sir William Forbes—merged since 1838 in the joint-stock Union Bank of Scotland—had a somewhat complicated genealogy, reaching far back in the last century—the century of progress in Scotland—and even faintly gleaming through the obscurities of the one before it, when mercantile efforts and speculations were taking their birth amidst the embers of scarcely extinct civil wars and all kinds of private barbarisms. The genealogy is here traced through a firm styled John Coutts & Co., of which the principal member was John Coutts, lord-provost of Edinburgh in the years 1742 and 1743, to Patrick Coutts, who carried on considerable merchandise at Montrose in the reign of William III. The concern is shewn as the main stock from which branched off the eminent London banking firms of Coutts & Co., Strand, and Herries & Co., St James's Street.

The earlier part of the narrative exhibits banking in its original condition as a graft upon ordinary merchandise. The goldsmith, the corn-merchant, the commission agent, were the first who gave bills of exchange or discounted private notes; and such were the only bankers known even in England till near the close of the seventeenth century. The house of John Coutts & Co. was entirely of this nature, and it had several rivals in Edinburgh. It is curious to trace the banking part of their business as rising, from a subordination to corn-dealing and other traffic, to be the principal, and finally the sole business, and to learn that the banker, in consequence of early connections, long continued to supply distant correspondents with articles which would now be ordered from the family grocer and oilman. It has strangely come about in our own time, that banking companies have, in some instances, been drawn once more into what might be called merchandise, or more properly mercantile speculation, in consequence of overgreat advances to private traffickers. But of this vice, which we have lately seen productive of such wide-spread ruin, there was little or no appearance during a long middle period embraced by this Memoir. And here lies, as the editor apprehends, one of the chief points of interest involved in the present volume. It depicts a banking-house limiting its transactions to its own proper sphere of business—yielding once or twice to temptations to do otherwise, and suffering from it, till at length it put on the fixed resolution *to be a banking-house only*, and neither directly nor indirectly a mercantile speculator, and thriving accordingly. The Memoir is, however, something more than this, for it exhibits a fine example of what prudence, care, and diligence may achieve with small means in one of the most exalted branches of commerce. None of the men concerned in raising up this bank were rich, and we have details shewing us that their transactions and profits were at first upon a very limited scale. But the business was conducted on an appropriate scale of frugality; the simple tradesman-virtues of probity, civility, and attention to business were sedulously cultivated. All extravagance and needless risk were avoided. The firm was accommodated in a floor of the President's Stairs in the Parliament Close, and one of the partners seems to have dwelt on 'the premises.' The whole affair thus reminding us not a little of those modest out-of-the-way banking-houses on the continent, which we have sometimes such difficulty in finding when we are in search of change for a circular note. These unostentatious merits, which we see every day raising humble traffickers to wealth and eminence, had precisely the same effect in the case of this banking-house. The well-descended Sir William tells the lesson with great simplicity and candour, and it is one which can never be repeated too often.

The writer of this Memoir was born in 1739, heir to a Nova Scotia baronetcy, which his father held without any means of supporting it, beyond his exertions as a member of the Scottish bar. Left fatherless at four years of age, he owed much in his early days to an amiable and intelligent mother, who contrived to maintain the style and manners of a lady on what would now be poverty in a much humbler grade of life. His career as a banker, from an apprenticeship entered upon at fifteen, till he became the head of an important house, and recovered all the fortunes lost or squandered by former generations of his family, is detailed in the work now laid before the public, along with much of the analogous progress made by the country during the same period. It remains to be mentioned that Sir William, in 1770, married a daughter of Dr James Hay of Hayston in Peeblesshire, and became the father of four sons, the eldest of whom, William, who succeeded him in the baronetcy, and died in 1828, is addressed in this Memoir; the second, John Hay Forbes, became a judge in the Court of Session, under the designation of Lord Medwyn; the third, Mr George Forbes, spent his life as a member of the banking-house; the youngest, Charles, was an officer in the navy. Sir William, in 1805, presented to the world a life of his friend Dr Beattie, which met a favourable reception, not merely as an elegant narration of the biography of an eminent man, but as preserving a great amount of the general literary history of the country which must have otherwise perished. He did not long outlive this effort, dying of water in the chest in November 1806, at the age of sixty-seven.

These are but the dry bones of a life distinguished in an extraordinary degree, not merely by energy and ability in professional affairs, but by ceaseless efforts of an enlightened character for the public good, by inexhaustible private charity, by high taste and refinement, and the practice of all the active virtues. One would need to have lived through the last fifty years in Scotland, to be fully aware of the excellences of various kinds which made people speak with such veneration of Sir William Forbes, and maintain a faith in his modest private bank such as is now scarcely given to the joint-stock of large copartneries. It was but participation in a universal feeling which caused Scott to thus refer to Sir William, in addressing one of the cantos of *Marmion* to the amiable banker's son-in-law and the poet's friend, Mr Skene of Rubislaw :

> 'Scarce had lamented Forbes paid
> The tribute to his Minstrel's shade,
> The tale of friendship scarce was told,
> Ere the narrator's heart was cold—
> Far may we search before we find
> A heart so manly and so kind !
> But not around his honoured urn
> Shall friends alone and kindred mourn ;
> The thousand eyes his care had dried,
> Pour at his name a bitter tide ;
> And frequent falls the grateful dew,
> For benefits the world ne'er knew.
> If mortal charity dare claim
> The Almighty's attributed name,
> Inscribe above his mouldering clay,
> "The widow's shield, the orphan's stay."
> Nor, though it wake thy sorrow, deem
> My verse intrudes on this sad theme ;
> For sacred was the pen that wrote,
> "Thy father's friend forget thou not."
> And grateful title may I plead
> For many a kindly word and deed,
> To bring my tribute to his grave :—
> 'Tis little—but 'tis all I have.'

And perhaps even a more expressive testimony is given to the character of Sir William by James Boswell, when he makes the following statement in his *Tour to the Hebrides:* 'Mr Scott came to breakfast, at which I introduced to Dr Johnson and him my friend Sir William Forbes, now of Pitsligo, a man of whom too much good cannot be said ; who, with distinguished abilities and application in his profession of a banker, is at once a good companion and a good Christian, which, I think, is saying enough. Yet it is but justice to record that once, when he was in a dangerous illness, he was watched with the anxious apprehension of a general calamity; day and night his house was beset with affectionate inquiries, and upon his recovery, *Te Deum* was the universal chorus from the hearts of his countrymen.'

R. C.

[ADDRESS OF THE AUTHOR TO HIS SON.]

EDINBURGH, 1st *January* 1803.

MY DEAREST WILLIAM,—

You have often heard me express an intention of writing some account of our house of business in Edinburgh, from its first establishment by the Messrs Coutts.

The history of a society in which I have passed the whole of my time, from my boyish days to this present hour, during the long period of almost half a century, cannot but be very interesting to me, especially since by means of my connection with it, I have arrived, through the blessing of Providence, to a degree of opulence and respectability of position, which I had very little reason to look for on my first entrance into the world. I have often thought that such a narrative might not be without its advantage to you, as calculated to teach you the necessity of prudence and caution in business of every kind, but most particularly in that of a banker, in whose possession not only his own property, but that of hundreds of others, is at stake; and as shewing you how, by a steady, well-concerted plan, with a strict adherence to integrity in all your transactions, aided by civility, yet without meanness, you can scarcely fail, by the blessing of Heaven, to arrive at success.

From such a history, too, some general knowledge may be gained of the progressive improvement of Scotland. For, although it is no doubt true that, even where things remain in a good measure stationary in a country, the business of a banking-house, the longer it exists, has a natural tendency to increase, when it has been conducted with prudence and ability, yet it is certainly to the rapid progress of the prosperity of this country, that the very great extension of the business of our house during the last twenty years must, in a great measure, be attributed. To illustrate this part of my proposed subject, I have subjoined to my narrative a short and, I must acknowledge, a very imperfect sketch, collected from the best authorities I could meet with; to some of which, my situation as a man of business has given me peculiar access. The subject is curious, and to me extremely interesting; as I have lived in the very period when this improvement of our native country has assumed some form, and seems still to be making daily advances to yet greater prosperity—a reflection highly grateful to me as a Scotsman.

To my own memory this narrative will recall many scenes on which I cannot look back without the most heartfelt gratitude to that Almighty Being, who has been graciously pleased to shower down upon me so large a share of prosperity. Nor can I contemplate the many years I have spent in business, and the number of friends of whom death has in that interval deprived me, without the most serious reflections on the rapidity with which this life is wearing away, and the propriety of my bending my thoughts towards another—a subject of meditation at all times proper for a rational being; but peculiarly so for one who has lived so long as I have done in the hurry and tumult of a constant intercourse with the busy world—a state extremely unfavourable to sober thought and reflection.

I cannot conclude this address to you, my dearest William, in a better manner than by expressing my hope that this narrative will confirm you in a love for that profession which you probably adopted at first on my suggestion. My wish certainly was to insure your succession to the fruits of my labours, as far as I have had any merit in helping to raise the house to its present flourishing state. If you continue to pay the same attention to business that I have done (I trust I may speak it in this place without vanity), I have no doubt that, by the blessing of Heaven on your endeavours, you may preserve the house in credit and respectability long after I shall have paid my debt to nature. But I never can too often nor too earnestly inculcate that the continuance of that credit and prosperity, under Providence, must entirely depend on yourself. If you prove yourself worthy of the notice of your father's friends (of which I must do you the justice to say, I have at this moment the fairest hope), you may expect their most cordial support, as well as a continuance of that favour and preference with which they have so long and so steadily honoured me. But if your own endeavours be wanting—if negligence take the place of attention to business, and economy be abandoned for profusion of expense—you may be assured that the concerns of the house will go speedily into decay, until at last that decline shall terminate in absolute ruin. For, in the course of a long experience, I can safely say that I have never known a single instance in which relaxed management and unbounded expense did not end in total bankruptcy.

That the providence of the Almighty may ever watch over you to shield you from harm, is the earnest and daily prayer of,

My dearest William,

Your fond and affectionate father,

WILLIAM FORBES.

MEMOIRS

OF A

BANKING-HOUSE.

THE founder of the Edinburgh house of business of which I am now to give some account, was *Patrick Coutts*, the fourth son of *Alexander Coutts*, provost of Montrose, whose grandfather is said to have been a son of the family of Auchintowl, and to have settled in Montrose in the end of the sixteenth century.*

At what period Mr Patrick Coutts removed from Montrose to Edinburgh I have not learned. But it appears by his books of accounts, still in our possession, that he carried on business in

---

* The pedigree of Mr Coutts has been thus stated to me by a letter from Mr Charles Thomson of Montrose, who had it from Mrs Patison, a relative of the family.

'The first of the family came to Montrose towards the end of the sixteenth century. He is said to have been a son of Coutts of Auchintowl, a vassal of the family of Macdonald. This gentleman had a son, William, who was provost of Montrose. William was succeeded by his son, Alexander, who lived to a great age, and left six sons and three daughters: of the sons, William, the eldest, was also provost of Montrose, as was likewise John, the second son; Hercules, the third, settled in London; Peter, the fourth, *settled in Edinburgh;* Robert, the fifth, went to America, and died there; James, the youngest, also went to America, but returned after some time, and purchased the lands of Hallgreen, in the shire of Kincardine, and was also provost of Montrose. This gentleman was the father of the late Mr Coutts of Hallgreen; and *Provost Coutts of Edinburgh* was the son of Peter, the fourth son of Alexander Coutts. I shall only add that I have had opportunity to learn that the family have been long and universally respected in Montrose as people of very great benevolence, honour, and integrity.' Of the truth of this last assertion there can be no better proof than that in three generations four of the family were elected chief magistrate of their native town.

Edinburgh as a merchant at least as early as the year 1696.* The books are kept in Scots money, and very neatly and distinctly written. He appears to have been a general merchant, whose transactions were considerably extended, for in his books there are accounts of mercantile adventures to New York and Pennsylvania, to Amsterdam, to France, and to the Canaries. He died in the autumn of 1704; his will being dated 25th July in that year, and an inventory of his effects registered in the books of the sheriff of Edinburgh on the 27th October thereafter. By the latter he appears to have left of personal estate somewhat better than £30,000 Scots, or £2500 sterling, a considerable sum for those days. Mr Patrick Coutts was twice married. He left three children—John, James, and Christian—by his first wife, a daughter of the family of Dunlop of Garnkirk, in the county of Lanark. This relationship gave rise to the intimate correspondence which always subsisted between the Messrs Coutts and the Messrs Dunlop and their connections in Glasgow. His second wife was Rachel Balfour, as appears from the record of the baptism of a daughter named Janet. After the death of Mr Patrick Coutts, his children of the first marriage were sent to Montrose, where they lived with an uncle from the year 1705 to 1719, when the eldest son, John, returned to Edinburgh. Mr John Coutts—who was born 28th July 1699—being a minor when his father died, I presume the business of the latter had been in a great degree discontinued by himself before his death, and wound up by the tutors

* [In the record of the Privy Council of Scotland, under date July 3, 1694, occurs a petition from Patrick Coutts, merchant in Montrose, who, acting for himself and partners, had bought a parcel of serges and worsted stuffs at Leeds, and had them shipped on board a Swedish vessel bound for Riga. The vessel was taken by a French privateer, and carried, with all its cargo, into Dunkirk. Coutts and his partners then represented to the Privy Council that it was customary in such cases to send a person to Dunkirk, who 'might recover the goods for a small price, as being English goods prohibited to be imported into the French dominions;' and they craved permission to send 'ane honest and weel-affected person' for that purpose, due security being given 'that he shall behave weel and honestly, without acting any thing against their majesties' government.'

The Council gave permission to Patrick himself 'to repair to Dunkirk, for recovering the goods mentioned, and from thence to undertake and perfect a voyage with the goods to any port within the kingdom of Scotland or England,' he having first taken the oath of allegiance, and given security to the extent of a thousand pounds sterling, that he should not consult or contrive anything against the government, 'nor carry any message by word or write in his going to or coming from France.'

These precautions bore reference to the exiled royal family residing at St Germains, and to the constant traffic carried on with it by Jacobite gentlemen of Scotland.]

John Coutts Esq.
LORD PROVOST of the CITY of EDINBURGH. 1742.
From a Painting by A. Ramsay.

he left to his children, for it does not appear that he had any partner by whom it might have been carried on.

With whom or where Mr John Coutts served an apprenticeship, or in what year he first commenced business as a merchant, I do not know. From some letters still existing, I find him engaged in mercantile concerns in Edinburgh in the year 1723. But most of his earliest books of accounts are lost, and his papers in much confusion. On the 23d of September 1730, he entered the town-council of Edinburgh as first merchant councillor. He married a sister of the late Sir John Stuart of Allanbank, by whom he had four sons—Patrick, John, James, and Thomas. At one period he was connected in partnership with Mr Haliburton of Newmains, in Roxburghshire,* but of the commencement or termination of that connection I can find no trace. In the year 1740, I find him in partnership with Mr Robert Ramsay, brother of Sir Alexander Ramsay of Balmain; from whom he separated on the 5th of December 1744, as appears by an entry in his journal, declaring that their partnership had terminated that day, and that he was thenceforward to carry on business alone. Afterwards, however, he assumed as a partner Mr Archibald Trotter, who was Mrs Coutts's first cousin,† and had been in the house of Charles and Hugh Smith of Boulogne. Both the first mentioned partnerships were under the firm of John Coutts & Co.; but this had the title of Coutts and Trotter. Their business was dealing in corn, buying and selling goods on commission, and the negotiation of bills of exchange on London, Holland, France, Italy, Spain, and Portugal. The negotiation of bills of exchange formed at that period a considerable part of the business of Edinburgh; for there were then no country banks, and consequently the bills for the exports and imports of Perth, Dundee, Montrose, Aberdeen, and other trading towns in Scotland, with Holland, France, and other countries, were negotiated at Edinburgh.‡ I see many notices of

* [Thomas Haliburton, of Newmains, living about that time, was, through a daughter, great-grandfather to Sir Walter Scott.]

† [Mr Archibald Trotter was the second son of Alexander Trotter of Castleshiel, by Jean, daughter of Sir Robert Stuart of Allanbank.]

‡ [In both sections of this island, for a long period after public banks were established, the negotiating of bills of exchange was in the hands of private merchants or bankers. 'The Bank [of Scotland], at its first erection, did deal in exchange, but found it very troublesome, unsafe, and improper. . . . There is no place in the trading world but there are to be found in it many that deal in exchange, even in those cities where a bank is. In London there are a great many, and those who have the management of the Bank of England never, that I have heard of, wished to rival them in their business. On the contrary, I am told that they help and accommodate them by discounting of bills, &c.'—*Account of the Bank of Scotland, printed about* 1727.]

the difficulty, at that time, of effecting money transactions of any considerable extent in the country towns of Scotland; a sure proof of the utility of provincial banks, which, when properly formed and judiciously conducted, are of the utmost benefit to the trade of the kingdom, and have been one great means, among others, of the opulence at which the country has arrived in the course of the last century,* as I have more particularly shewn in another place.

By the death of his brother, James Coutts, a merchant in London, he succeeded to about £20,000, which was deemed a large fortune in those days; and being a man of high character as a merchant, as well as of very popular and agreeable manners, he lived with a degree of hospitality and expense not usual in the family of a merchant at that period. He is reported to have been the first lord provost of Edinburgh who did the honours of the city, by entertaining strangers in his own house; it having generally been the custom that all such entertainments were given in a tavern at the city's expense. Unfortunately, he was thus led into excesses of the table, and other indulgences, which at length hurt his constitution; so that, falling into bad health, he left the charge of the business of his house and of his two youngest sons—the second being in Holland—to his partner, Mr Trotter, and, taking his eldest son Patrick along with him as a companion, he set out for Italy on the 8th August 1749. A few days before his departure, he executed a new contract of copartnery with Mr Trotter, in which the partners were himself, his eldest son Patrick, and Mr Trotter, under the firm of Coutts, Son, and Trotter. The stock of this company was £4000 sterling. He died at Nola, near Naples, on the 23d March 1750, at the age of fifty-one, beloved and regretted by all his acquaintance, who overlooked the imperfections of his character when they thought of him as the upright citizen and useful magistrate, ever zealous in the service of his friends, and a most agreeable member of society. I give this character of Provost Coutts from what I have been told by those who were of his personal acquaintance, for I had not myself the opportunity of knowing him, as he was dead before I came to Edinburgh. By the death of Provost Coutts, his sons being all under age, the executive part of the business devolved

* [In 1803, the three public banks of Edinburgh had *thirty-nine* branches throughout the country, and it is believed there were very few other provincial banking establishments then in existence. The *Edinburgh Almanac* for 1858 gives a list of *three hundred and sixty-six* branches from the Edinburgh banks, besides two banks in Glasgow and six in the other towns, having *a hundred and ninety-five* branches.]

on Mr Trotter. After a few years, however, the young gentlemen and he not agreeing together, Mr Trotter resigned his share in the company. He, I have understood, differed widely in his character from Provost Coutts, not possessing that liberality of thinking and acting in business for which the latter was so greatly distinguished. The young gentlemen seem to have considered him more in the light of a governor than a partner; and as neither his person nor manners were at all calculated to command their respect, his young friends were constantly teasing him with little boyish, roguish tricks. One that I remember hearing of, when I entered the office, consisted in their putting a live mouse under the cover of his inkstand, and watching with glee for the start he was to give, when, on his lifting the lid, the animal jumped out, to the no small amusement, as might be expected, of the whole counting-house.*

* After Mr Trotter left the copartnery, he tried to establish himself in business as an accountant, for which he was ill qualified, and as an arbitrator in mercantile disputes. He afterwards accepted the rather ungracious office of agent for certain Edinburgh banks in their warfare with those of Glasgow, to which place he occasionally repaired to make demands for gold. At times he was subject to a species of religious melancholy, which he inherited from his mother, the Lady Castleshiels of the Allanbank family—by whom he was related to the Messrs Coutts. She had composed a most extraordinary *Book of Meditations*, which her son published some little time before his death. He at last retired from all business, and resided at an estate in the neighbourhood of Edinburgh, which he obtained by his wife.

[The warfare here alluded to by Sir William was of a peculiar character. The Royal Bank of Scotland, from its commencement, in 1727, had been favoured and supported by the merchants of Glasgow. There was a great deal of angry rivalry between that establishment and its senior, the Bank of Scotland, which had considered itself extremely ill-used by the government of George I., when the Royal Bank obtained its charter. The bad blood found expression in proceedings which no Scottish bank would now dream of condescending to, but which were then considered quite legitimate; at least they were very common. The banks would hoard up a quantity of each other's notes, and endeavour, by presenting them suddenly, to create embarrassment. To counteract the bias of the Glasgow merchants for the Royal Bank, the Bank of Scotland took part, in 1749, in establishing what was afterwards known as the *Old Bank* in the western city. As a protective or retaliatory measure, the Royal Bank helped next year in setting up the New Banking Company at Glasgow. From the papers connected with the case 'Archibald Trotter v. Andrew Cochrane, John Murdoch & Co.,' it appears that, some years afterwards, the Edinburgh banks became sensible of a common injury from these western establishments, and laid aside their old animosities in order to get them, if possible, put down. They concurred in calling upon the Glasgow merchants to give up the trade of banking, under the pain of having their credits withdrawn. This was refused, and then it was that Mr Trotter, in order to further the objects of the Edinburgh banks and distress the west country bankers, took up his residence in Glasgow.

'Mr Trotter certainly made a practice of receiving, or rather of collecting the notes, of Murdoch & Co., and demanding payment of large sums in cash; and

On Mr Trotter's leaving them, as they were too young to conduct a house of business by themselves, their friends formed a new copartnery for them with Mr John Stephen, who had been married to a sister of their father, and was at that time a wine-merchant in Leith, in company with the Honourable Alexander Stuart, afterwards Lord Blantyre, and a Mr Walter Scott. On this occasion the firm of the house was changed to Coutts Brothers & Co.

A mercantile establishment was likewise formed about this time in London, by the Messrs Coutts, under the firm of Coutts,

Murdoch & Co. resorted to the practice of telling out payment very deliberately indeed, in sixpences. In a protest which he took upon 23d January 1759, he gives a detail of the payments which were thus obtained by him from 14th December to 22d January (thirty-four business days), amounting altogether only to the sum of £2893. One of the forenoon payments in sixpences amounted only to £7; and the highest, either of a forenoon or afternoon (for business was then done after dinner), is £20. The largest payment made, which was in Edinburgh notes, was one of £100.

'Mr Trotter, in his action before the Court of Session, sought decree for £3447, to which extent he held notes of Murdoch & Co., with interest on the amount of notes held by him at the date of his protest, with £600 damages. He also sought to have it declared that Murdoch & Co. had no right to regulate their own hours of doing business, and that they should be bound to pay their notes when presented at any time from seven morning to ten at night.

'The defences stated were, that Mr Trotter had acted *in mala fide*, and with the design of distressing the defendants; that his conduct might be strictly legal; but so was that of the defendants strictly legal in paying in sixpences, a practice which, on occasions, had been resorted to by the Edinburgh banks themselves; that payment had nevertheless been offered, but refused, unless damages were also paid; and that the declarator as to hours was not competent at the instance of a private party. A great many dilatory proceedings took place before the Lord Ordinary (Woodhall), who ultimately ordered informations. In June 1760, a petition and complaint was presented by Mr Trotter, complaining of his adversaries for trifling with justice. The information for the defendants having been lodged, the Court, on advising, remitted to the Lord Ordinary to adjust the facts—and especially the fact of Mr Trotter's being a mere hand for the banks, and his intention to distress, which several of the judges thought obvious. Lord Kames observed, that Mr Trotter should not have taken the notes. Lord Affleck thought the case of Mr Trotter's like that of a man's buying up another's debts *in malitia*. The Lord President and Lord Coalston dreaded paper credit, and thought banks dangerous. A great variety of proceedings again took place before the Lord Ordinary, who again ordered pleadings to the whole Court. In December 1761, the libel was held relevant to infer the conclusions for payment of principal, interest, and expenses, but not as to declaratory conclusions. Kames, Nisbet, and Affleck were against the interlocutor. Coalston and Edgefield declined as directors of the bank. There was then a petition for Mr Trotter, with answers and replies. Then two petitions for Murdoch & Co., with answers, &c.; and in April 1763, the case was taken out of Court by the defendants paying £600—to which, we have no doubt, the pursuer's expenses had by that time amounted, and by which time also, we have no doubt, Murdoch & Co. had accomplished their object in defending the action.'—*Scotsman newspaper, April 5, 1826.*]

Stephen, Coutts, & Co., in which Mr Thomas Stephen, their cousin-german, the son of the partner at Edinburgh, was concerned. That company acted as the correspondents of the house at Edinburgh, and transacted any other business with which they were intrusted, either in money or in the buying and selling of goods on commission.

Mr Patrick and Mr Thomas Coutts resided with Mr Thomas Stephen, in the house occupied by the London firm, in Jeffrey's Square, St Mary Axe, and conducted the business there, while the other two brothers, John (who not long after his father's death withdrew from his mercantile concern in Rotterdam* and returned to Scotland) and James, resided at Edinburgh, conducting the business of the house there, in conjunction with the elder Mr Stephen. They lived in the same house which their father had inhabited, being the second floor of the President's Stairs in the Parliament Close; and they continued in the same line of business of banking and exchange which their father had carried on. Like him, too, they dealt very largely in corn; and it is not without some degree of wonder that I look back on the extent of their correspondence and operations in that article. They had a settled agent in Northumberland, William Watson, residing at Fenwick, who was employed to make purchases of corn for the house (and for none else) in that county. Messrs Fairholme, Mr Chalmers, and other corn-dealers in Edinburgh, had established agents in the same fertile district—employing Fenwick, moreover, to make purchases for them in Berwickshire. George Garioch at Aberdeen, James Robertson at Portsoy, and Andrew Laird at Dundee, made purchases (in which these gentlemen were themselves concerned) for the house in the fertile corn counties of Perth, Forfar, Kincardine, Aberdeen, Banff, and Moray; and James Budge of Toftingall in Caithness, and William Baillie of Rosehall in Ross-shire, both of them gentlemen of landed property, but also men of business, though not strictly speaking merchants, made purchases for the house on their joint account in those northern counties. In England the house had large quantities of corn shipped for them at Yarne and at Stockton, in Yorkshire; at Lynn Regis, Fakenham, and Yarmouth, all in the rich corn county of Norfolk; at Haverfordwest, in South Wales; and by the noted Cooper Thornhill, who

---

* The firm of the Rotterdam house was Robertson, Coutts, and Strachan. Their chief trade was the shipping of tea, spirits, and other articles of contraband goods, for the smugglers on the east and north coasts of Scotland. His friends at Edinburgh, disliking this trade, procured a separation between him and his partners in Holland, very fortunately for Mr Coutts, as that house became bankrupt a very few years afterwards.

at that time kept the Bell Inn at Hilton, and was one of the most considerable corn-factors in England.*

They had also large dealings in corn with Edmund and George Schoales of Drogheda, and with Daniel Mussenden of Belfast;† and I have known them import cargoes of wheat from Dantzic and Königsberg. When I reflect on the extent of all this correspondence, and the combination of such a variety of intelligence respecting the prices of corn at all those different places, compared with the prices in the different parts of Scotland, I cannot but wonder at the boldness of enterprise which led them to embark in such a perilous traffic. Some years they made large profits, which they as often lost in others, owing to the fluctuation of markets and the bankruptcy of many of those with whom they dealt. Indeed, I have often thought it not a little singular that a banking-house, which, of all branches of business, seems peculiarly to require caution, and which ought, as much as possible, to be kept clear of every undertaking of hazard or speculation, should have chosen to embark so largely in the corn-trade, which is perhaps that most liable to sudden fluctuation, and in which no human prudence or insurance can guard the adventurers from frequent loss. Yet in this the Messrs Coutts were not singular. Messrs Fairholme, whose banking-house had been long eminent, and in the enjoyment of unsullied credit, were also large dealers in corn. George Chalmers, whose principal employment was that of a corn-dealer, also did business as a banker and exchange-dealer.

* It was he who performed the extraordinary ride from Hilton to London, back to Hilton, and thence to London again, being 225 miles, in 12 hours 17 minutes. He set out at four o'clock in the morning of 29th April 1745, and came to the Queen's Arms, opposite Shoreditch Church, in 3 hours and 52 minutes; returned again to Hilton in 4 hours and 12 minutes; and came back to London in 4 hours and 13 minutes. He was allowed 15 hours for the task and as many horses as he pleased, which he had ready waiting him at various places on the road. He was so little fatigued by this exploit, that he rode next day as if nothing had happened. The road was lined with spectators to see him pass and repass, and many thousands, besides his own wager of five hundred guineas, were depending on the performance. Mr Thornhill, though he kept an inn, was much respected for his gentleman-like manners, and generally brought to table by his guests. There is a mezzotinto print of this exploit still preserved at the Bell Inn at Hilton.

† I recollect a singular circumstance respecting Daniel Mussenden, who was one of the most eminent corn-dealers in the north of Ireland. His business had been long conducted, under his inspection, by a confidential clerk, who wrote all his letters, excepting only the signature. At length his faculties became so impaired, that this clerk not only managed the business and wrote the letters, but imitated his master's subscription at the bottom of the letters, and in all his bills, so exactly, that no difference could be detected, although, as I well recollect, Mr Mussenden's subscription was a very peculiar one.

Fordyce, Malcolm, & Co., Arbuthnot and Guthrie, Gibson and Hogg, and some others, were all established afterwards on the same footing.

The other principal banking-houses in Edinburgh at that time were Messrs Mansfield & Co., William Cuming, William Hogg and Son, and William Alexander and Sons. The two first confined themselves strictly to the banking business, in which they rose to great eminence from a very obscure origin. From a slender outsetting as a draper, old Mr James Mansfield began to deal a little in bills of exchange, and by degrees founded a banking-house of the first celebrity in Scotland.* In the same manner William Cuming succeeded to his father, old Patrick Cuming's cloth shop in the Parliament Close, which he afterwards converted into a counting-house, where he confined himself entirely to the transacting of money business, and after a long life, left a very large fortune. William Hogg and Son were not in very extensive business, and they managed it very confusedly. William Alexander and Sons were very considerable money-dealers, though their chief employment was the purchasing tobacco for the farmers-general of France. A few years afterwards, a number of other inconsiderable houses started up, who transacted money business—such as Samuel Foggo, Johnstone and Smith, Scott Moncreiffe and Ferguson, John Fyffe, and W. Sinclair & Co.—most of whom, along with several of those formerly mentioned, became bankrupt in the famous year 1772.† Thomas Kinnear was originally an insurance-broker, but laid the foundation of a banking-house of eminence, afterwards carried on by his sons. Seton and Houstoun sprang out of a society who dealt in the manufacturing of woollen goods.

It was somewhat uncommon to see a whole family, consisting of four sons, all carrying on the succession of their father's house in a joint partnership of business with success. Those brothers, however, were not all of the same temper and disposition. Patrick, the eldest son of Provost Coutts, was a man of elegant and agreeable manners, but more inclined to the study of books than to

---

* [Mansfield, Ramsay, & Co., continued to be an eminent banking firm in Edinburgh till 1807, after which the house appears under the appellative of Ramsays, Bonars, & Co.]

† John Fyffe, from a principle of high honour, suspended his payments in 1772, because he was fearful of the effect of those numerous bankruptcies which he saw daily happening around him. But, on a more narrow inspection of his affairs, he found no reason for apprehension, and very soon went on again. He was a worthy honest man, of great respectability, and lived long retired from business. He died after 1790, leaving an ample fortune to his family.

application to business. He continued, however, to take a part in the management of the London establishment for some few years, in the course of which Mr Thomas Stephen died, and the active charge of the counting-house chiefly rested with the youngest brother Thomas. Patrick Coutts then spent some time in travelling on the continent, where a very unpleasant accident befell him. Being at Lisle, as he was walking in a careless manner on the ramparts, he was observed to be employed in taking notes in shorthand in his pocket-book, and was immediately arrested as a spy. It was in vain that he urged his having merely been engaged in making a few memoranda for his own amusement, without any criminal intention. He was thrown into prison, where he remained for several months, and it cost his friends considerable trouble to procure his release. He afterwards came home, and paid a visit to Scotland, when I had the opportunity of becoming in a slight degree acquainted with him, and he is a party to the first contract I entered into with him and his brothers and Mr Stephen, by which I became entitled to a small interest in the house of Coutts Brothers & Co. Afterwards returning to London, he was attacked by a direful malady, which he inherited from his mother's family. He is still (1803) alive, above seventy years of age.

John Coutts, the second son, under whose eye chiefly I served my apprenticeship, was one of the most agreeable men I ever knew. Lively and well-bred, and of very engaging manners, he had the happy talent of uniting a love of society and public amusements with a strict attention to business. While resembling his father in his general manners more than did any of his brothers, he was more correct in his conduct; nor do I recollect to have ever seen him but once in the counting-house disguised with liquor and incapable of transacting business.* Having received his mercantile education in Holland, he had all the accuracy and all the strictness of a Dutchman; and to his lessons it is that I owe any knowledge I possess of the principles of business, as well as an attachment to *form*, which I shall probably carry with me to the grave. Although he was of the most gentle manners in common life, he was easily heated with passion when he thought himself ill-used, and I have seen his eyes, which were black and piercing, flash as with lightning, if any attempt was made to overreach him in a bargain. But his passion was of short continuance, and easily appeased.

* [We must accept this fact, and the evident simplicity and good feeling under which the author mentions it, as illustrations of the manners of past times. It clearly appears that in Sir William's time, while invariable sobriety might be esteemed, an occasional occurrence of the reverse was not deemed fatal to a man of business.]

He was seized, in London, with the severe disorder called iliac passion, and, going to Bath for the recovery of his health, he died there on the 4th of August 1761—I believe, in the thirtieth year of his age. I shall ever retain the most grateful respect for his memory, on account of the very great attention he bestowed on me during the five years of my apprenticeship.

Mr James Coutts gave as close application to business as his immediate elder brother; but he was by no means of so amiable a character; and, never having been out of Edinburgh, he had not those polished manners which his two elder brothers had acquired by living abroad and mixing in the world. He was nearly as passionate as Mr John Coutts; but he differed from him in retaining a longer resentment. As he went to London, and by his marriage became established there in business after I came into the counting-house, I was but a few months under his care; so that it was not till I grew up to be a man that I enjoyed much of his acquaintance. The unhappy difference which took place between him and my partners on the subject of Mr William Cochrane, in which I was unfortunately involved, occasioned a coolness between him and them. But I must do Mr James Coutts the justice to say, that, even after that period, he always behaved to me with kindness and attention. At last an unhappy difference arose between him and his youngest brother Thomas, whom he had assumed as a partner, which ended in their final separation. In consequence of that event, Mr James Coutts went abroad with his daughter, an only child, accompanied by a female relative as her companion. At Turin he was seized with the same malady as his eldest brother, of which he had previously shewn symptoms, but which attacked him in a different manner. It was thought expedient that he should go home by sea, and the vessel having touched at Gibraltar, he died there, early in the year 1778.

Of Mr Thomas Coutts, the youngest son of Provost Coutts, as he is still (1803) alive and in business, it is not proper to say much. I may just remark that, by a careful attention to the business of a banker, he has raised the reputation and business of his house to a high degree of eminence, and has acquired a very great fortune.*

Mr [Francis] Farquharson [of Haughton] had been my father's most intimate friend and companion from a very early period, and

---

* [The well-known Thomas Coutts, after attaining to be the head of his distinguished profession in London, and acquiring enormous wealth, died in February 1822, about the age of ninety.]

although not in the nomination of my guardians, his high regard for my father had attached him strongly to my mother and her infant children, to whom he proved himself a steady and most useful friend to his dying hour. The slender provision which my father had left me—although he had by great attention to business and frugality been enabled in the course of his short life to double the pittance which originally fell to him out of the wreck of our family estate, when sold by his grandfather—having rendered it absolutely necessary that I should attach myself to some profession for my future support, Mr Farquharson suggested to my mother the propriety of breeding me to commercial business, in preference to any of the learned professions, as a surer road to independence. In prosecution of this plan, after my education in the usual branches of school learning was completed, he prevailed on his young friends, the Messrs Coutts, to receive me as an apprentice into their counting-house, the circumstance to which, by the blessing of Heaven, I owe that respectable situation in life to which I have attained.

At this period, as I have already said, Messrs Coutts carried on business both at Edinburgh and London—at Edinburgh, under the firm of Coutts Brothers & Co., conducted by John and James Coutts and Mr Stephen; at London, under the firm of Coutts, Stephen, Coutts, & Co., conducted by Patrick and Thomas Coutts. The business at Edinburgh* comprised extensive transactions in corn on their own account. They also did business on commission, in the sale of wines and other consignments, and in shipping lead, salmon, and other articles; and, lastly, they acted as exchange dealers and bankers by receiving deposits of money, for which they allowed interest. The house in London was the correspondent of the house in Edinburgh, which conducted through them all their exchange operations, and they also transacted business both in buying and selling goods on commission.

In the month of August 1751, Mr James Coutts, who had never been out of Scotland, went to London on a visit to his brothers. There he very soon afterwards married Miss Polly Peagrim, the niece of George Campbell, an eminent banker in the

* The whole office staff, besides the partners, then comprised only four clerks and two apprentices including myself. I cannot omit mentioning, that, the year after myself, we were joined by Mr Lewis Hay, and the year following by Mr Hunter, afterwards Sir James Hunter Blair, who both became partners and my most intimate friends. In the same manner Mr Bartlet came into the house as a clerk in 177-, and my brother-in-law, Mr John Hay, in 1778, and you, my dear William, became an apprentice in 1788, and have since all been partners in the house.

Strand,* by whom he was immediately received into partnership, under the firm of Campbell and Coutts, and he in consequence withdrew from the partnerships with his brothers in London and Edinburgh.

Some short time afterwards, Mr William Dalrymple, merchant in Cadiz—brother of Sir Hew Dalrymple of North Berwick—was assumed as an acting partner in the house at London, the firm of which was then changed to Coutts Brothers and Dalrymple. In a very short time, however, Messrs Coutts disliking Mr Dalrymple's too great love of speculation, the partnership between them was dissolved by mutual consent,† and the firm was again changed to Coutts Brothers & Co., being the same with that of the Edinburgh house.

About the year 1760, Mr George Campbell, the banker, dying, Mr James Coutts assumed his youngest brother, Thomas, as a partner in that banking-house, the firm of which then became James and Thomas Coutts. In consequence, Thomas also withdrew from the two houses of Edinburgh and London, the last of which was thereafter managed by Mr Patrick Coutts, with the assistance of Mr Thomas Walker, their principal and confidential clerk, who had been originally bred in the counting-house at Edinburgh. Some difference having arisen between Mr Walker and them, he quitted their service; and a procuration was then given to Mr George Keith, who had been bred with Mr A. Gregory of Dunkirk, and had been recommended to Messrs Coutts as a clerk in their London establishment. Mr John Coutts and Mr Stephen continued to conduct the business of the house at Edinburgh.

While those changes were so rapidly succeeding each other, my apprenticeship of five years was completed on the 14th May 1759. Mr Francis Farquharson, my much esteemed friend, having

---

* At that period there were only two banking-houses on the west side of Temple Bar. One was the well-known establishment of Mr Andrew Drummond, a son of Lord Strathallan,¹ who, after having been engaged in the affair of 1715 on the side of the Stuart family, established himself as a banker in London, where he was patronised by many of the Tory families of the English aristocracy. George Campbell, the proprietor of the other establishment, was originally a goldsmith in London—as most of the bankers had been originally—and was patronised by the Duke of Argyle and the Whig interest.

† Mr Dalrymple, after his separation from Messrs Coutts, commenced business in London by himself, chiefly as an underwriter, but failed in a few months.

---

¹ [Mr Andrew Drummond, the banker, was only the son of Sir John Drummond of Machany; but his elder brother, William, succeeded as fourth Viscount Strathallan, and was killed fighting on the Prince's side at Culloden.]

it greatly at heart to procure for me an interest in the house at Edinburgh, advised me to continue to serve the company in the capacity of a clerk after my apprenticeship was finished, which I did for very nearly two years, without receiving any emolument, in the expectation of being at some convenient opportunity, through his means, admitted a partner.* On the 6th of August 1760, I was intrusted with a power of attorney, by which I was enabled to take an active part in the conducting of the business of the house; and Mr John Coutts with much kindness took every opportunity of bringing me into notice, by inviting me to dinner occasionally when he had parties of friends at his house. I take pleasure in mentioning this circumstance, though trivial in itself, as a grateful testimony of his goodness to me on every occasion. At length, a new contract for ten years having been executed by Mr Patrick Coutts, Mr John Coutts, and Mr Stephen, commencing 1st January 1761, an agreement was entered into between them and me on the 13th March 1761, by which I was to be concerned to the extent of one-eighth share of the house at Edinburgh. But so jealous were they of the effects of this concession in my favour, that the agreement was only to last for three years, with a power to any of them to put an end to it at the end of one year, if they should judge it expedient, and without permitting me to appear to the world in the character of a partner; so that I still continued to act by virtue of the power of attorney. These prudential restrictions on the part of Messrs Coutts might perhaps be deemed a little hard, as they had had a seven years' experience of my close application to business and zeal for their interest; yet they were cheerfully submitted to by me, with the hope of one day becoming an ostensible partner.

A few months after the execution of this agreement, Mr Patrick Coutts was laid aside from business by bad health, which ended in a deprivation of reason; and in the course of that summer, Mr John Coutts was seized at London with a painful disease, which brought him to the gates of death, and so broke his constitution, that, being ordered by his physicians to drink the waters of Bath, he died there in August 1761, deeply lamented by all who knew him, but by none more than by myself, who lost in him an able guide and a steady friend. By this unlooked-for stroke, the two houses of London and Edinburgh were left in a

---

* So strict was Mr John Coutts in the discipline of the counting-house, that I slept but one night out of Edinburgh from the commencement of my apprenticeship in May 1754 till the month of September 1760, when I obtained leave to go to Aberdeenshire with my mother, to pay a visit to our relations.

most destitute situation. The business of the house at London was of itself noway considerable; but it became of importance to the general interest by their being the correspondents of the house at Edinburgh, who drew their bills on them, and transacted through them their exchange business. The London house had not a person in it who was entitled to sign the firm, and although the business was very well attended to by Mr Keith, who held the company's power of attorney, it was impossible that he could have the weight of a partner, and it is wonderful that things went on so well as they did. At Edinburgh, matters were, if possible, still worse; as there was no ostensible partner but Mr Stephen, whose slender abilities were altogether inadequate to the task of conducting the houses, and for which my youth and inexperience rendered me extremely ill qualified. It was therefore a singular instance of the goodness of Providence to us, that, under such feeble management, the houses still supported their credit and reputation. Indeed, I must chiefly attribute it, under Heaven, to the popularity of Provost Coutts and his family in Edinburgh, and the established reputation of their firm, by which the friends and correspondents of the house were induced to continue their business there as formerly. Yet even that advantage would not have been sufficient, had I not been strongly supported and assisted by my intimate friend and companion, Mr Hunter, whom I have mentioned as my fellow-apprentice in the house. Although he was nearly two years younger than me, yet such were his superior abilities, that, through him alone, I may say, it was owing that Mr Stephen and I did not sink under the load of conducting a banking-house such as ours, inconsiderable as the business then was compared with what it has since become. Even then, however, the house was one of the first reputation in Edinburgh, for, of course, everything must be estimated by comparison. The first resolution which Mr Hunter and I formed, on finding ourselves practically the sole conductors of the house, was to wind up the corn-speculations then existing, and to relinquish that trade entirely, so as in future to confine the house to its proper and natural business of exchange and banking, by which prudent resolution, and by unremitting assiduity and attention, we were enabled to go on without any apparent diminution of business.

But to return from this digression, as Messrs James and Thomas Coutts, the only two brothers remaining capable of doing business, were bankers in London, and their eldest brother having fortune sufficient for his requirements in his retired mode of life, they would probably have given themselves little trouble about

the future continuance of the houses, had they not been desirous
of preserving them for the sake of their uncle-in-law, Mr Stephen,
as well as for rendering them subservient as a provision for
another uncle-in-law, Mr William Cochrane, married to their
mother's sister,* who was still alive, and to whom they were much
attached. They were besides, indeed, not without a personal
pecuniary interest in the question, what was to become of the
houses. For, as Messrs James and Thomas Coutts were the
representatives of their two elder brothers, Patrick and John,
they were, in fact, responsible for the current engagements of the
houses, and they also had at stake a large sum of outstanding
debts, which could noway be so effectually recovered as by continuing the houses under a new set of partners. Among these
outstanding debts was one of considerable amount owing by Mr
Stephen himself, who, never having had any capital stock of his
own, and having been occasionally forced to draw money from the
house for the payment of debts he had contracted in his mercantile
concerns before he was connected with it, was now its debtor
for a considerable balance. Mr Cochrane had been originally a
woollen-draper in the Luckenbooths, Edinburgh, in partnership
with Mr Walter Hamilton, but had been some time retired from
business, living on a small estate in the neighbourhood of
North Berwick. He was a man of honourable character and
agreeable manners, but altogether unacquainted with any
species of business beyond that of the retail shop in which
he had acted. Mr Stephen, as I have said, was a man of
the most slender abilities; and Mr Hunter and I were both
of us too young and too little known in the world to be solely
trusted to for conducting the house at Edinburgh, while that of
London stood still more in need of an able head. It naturally
occurred, therefore, to Messrs Coutts, that, if they meant at all to
preserve the two houses from sinking into insignificance, and
render them of any value as a provision for Mr Stephen and Mr
Cochrane, it was absolutely necessary that some new arrangement
should be formed, and some persons of established reputation and
abilities be found who might be associated with the others, and
might conduct the business on a plan that should promise success.
Some occasional correspondence with this view had taken place
with Messrs Coutts, but without anything decisive being resolved
on. Finding little progress made, therefore, towards such a
consummation, and having as a separate inducement a violent
desire to visit London, I obtained Messrs Coutts's permission to

* [Lillias, daughter of Sir John Stuart of Allanbank, Bart.]

repair thither in the end of October 1762, it having been previously agreed between Mr Hunter and me, that I should use the influence I had with Messrs Coutts to procure for him, if possible, an interest in any new arrangement that might be thought of—a measure on which I was of myself most anxiously bent, not only from my partiality to Mr Hunter, with whom I had lived six years in the strictest and most endearing intimacy, but from my consciousness of his superior abilities, and how very necessary it was that he should have an active and efficient share in the management, which, however, I could not look for on any other footing than as a partner; because, having inherited from his father a patrimony of £5000, he would naturally look out for some other establishment if he should see no prospect of being received into ours.

On my arrival in London, Messrs Coutts received me with much cordiality, and I remained there nearly two months, during which time I repeatedly urged the necessity of making some speedy arrangement. At length they informed me that, after mature deliberation, the person they had fixed on to be assumed as an active partner was Mr Robert Herries, merchant in Barcelona, at that time in London. Mr Herries was the eldest son of John Herries of Halldykes, a gentleman of a small landed property in Dumfriesshire, whose affairs becoming embarrassed, his son went at an early age to Rotterdam, where two brothers of his father, Robert and Charles Herries, were established as merchants, and with whom he served an apprenticeship. His eldest uncle, Robert, of whom I shall have afterwards much occasion to speak, having acquired what was considered in those days a competent fortune, withdrew from business, and returned to his own country, where he purchased from his eldest brother the family estate of Halldykes. Charles, the other brother, having fallen into habits of dissipation, his nephew Robert, notwithstanding the tempting offers made to him by his uncle, resolved to leave him; and having by his prudence and good conduct acquired many useful friends, particularly Messrs Hope & Co. of Amsterdam, he had been encouraged by them, and under their protection, though then not above three-and-twenty years of age, to establish himself as a merchant at Barcelona. One of the chief branches of the trade there consisted in shipping brandies made from the wines of the country; and as that trade was carried on to a very considerable extent in the Isle of Man, then the property of the Duke of Atholl, and where Mr Herries had the opportunity of forming many connections, Barcelona was for him a most eligible situation. He accordingly established himself there in the year 1754, and by his skilful management, under such powerful patronage, his house quickly rose to distinguished eminence. Having assumed into partnership a Prussian gentleman of the name of Tillebien, whom he had carried with him from Rotterdam as a clerk, and having brought his two younger brothers, Charles and William, to Barcelona, where he had educated them in business, he had come to Britain to pay a visit to his friends, and increase the number of his employers. His reputation as a man of abilities and credit not only stood high in the mercantile world, but his private character was distinguished as a son and a brother, who was in fact the support of his family; so that he seemed well qualified to preside over the two houses of London and Edinburgh. If anything was to be objected to him, it was his having too great a love for a variety of partnerships, as, in fact, besides his house at Barcelona, he had joined in establishing another at Montpellier, under the firm of Herries, Roy, and Burnet; and he had also a concern in the house of Honorius Dallio & Co. of Valencia. From all these, however, he declared himself resolved to withdraw, except from that of Barcelona, and he stipulated for a permission occasionally to visit Spain.

Mr Herries having lived at Rotterdam at the same period with Mr John Coutts, they had been intimate friends and companions; and it was while on a visit to Mr Coutts at Edinburgh, in the year 1761, that I had first the pleasure of making his acquaintance, which I renewed on my going to London at this time, when I had frequent opportunities of being in his company at the house of Messrs Coutts. His character and manners being therefore well known to me, I most readily assented for myself and Mr Hunter (who was now to have a share in the business) to assume Mr Herries a partner into the two houses, as Messrs Coutts did for Mr Stephen; and in consequence, articles of copartnery were drawn up in London, and signed by Mr Herries, Mr Cochrane (who was at that time in London on a visit to Messrs Coutts), and me, in Mr James Coutts's house in the Strand, on the evening of Christmas Day 1762. By those articles, the firm at Edinburgh was to be John Coutts & Co., out of respect to the memory of Provost Coutts; and the firm at London was to be Herries, Cochrane, & Co., Mr Herries and Mr Cochrane being the resident partners. Messrs Coutts were to give a loan of £7000, for seven years, of their eldest brother's money, in consideration of an allowance of 10 per cent., to be paid to him by the partners; and the contracts were to endure for twelve years, with a break at the end of every third year. The only unusual clause was a power which Messrs Coutts reserved to themselves, in the event of a vacancy happening, to bring in a new partner, in which event, however, any of the partners, if he disliked the new associate, was to be at liberty to withdraw from the society. To this privilege reserved to themselves by Messrs Coutts, Mr Herries strongly objected at the time, assigning as a reason that, as he would not allow any man to choose a wife for him, he had an equal dislike to a partner being chosen for him by anybody but himself. The article, however, was unfortunately suffered to stand a part of the agreement; and it was afterwards the cause of much dispute and altercation between Messrs Coutts and us. On the morning after signing the contract in London, Mr James Coutts, Mr Herries, and I set out for Scotland, in order to complete the contracts, and make the necessary preparations for the commencement of the new copartneries; and the new firms began to be used on the 1st February 1763. The counting-house at Edinburgh was continued in Provost Coutts's house in the President's Stairs, Parliament Close, in which Mr Stephen's family had resided since the death of Mr John Coutts. In London, the counting-house was also continued in the house where it had been first established, in Jeffrey's Square, St Mary Axe, in which Mr Patrick and Mr Thomas Coutts had resided, and which was now occupied by Mr and Mrs Cochrane.

The declared patronage of Messrs Coutts, who were bankers of eminence in London, the circumstance of James being member of parliament for the city of Edinburgh, the popularity of the name of John Coutts, and the established reputation of Mr Herries, all combined to give an additional degree of credit and respectability to the two houses, which it was the study of Mr Hunter and myself to increase by our unremitting attention to the executive part of the business. It was resolved by all concerned that the house at Edinburgh should totally abstain from dealing in corn or any other species of merchandise; confining themselves solely to their regular business of receiving money on deposit, granting cash-accounts, discounting bills, and dealing in exchanges on London, Holland, and France—a resolution to the adherence to which the great prosperity of the house may, under Heaven, be mainly attributed. It was also resolved that the house in London should chiefly confine itself to the sale and purchase of goods on commission and the business of exchanges.

On this footing, our new copartnery commenced, and the success was fully equal to our most sanguine expectations. The Seven

Years' War had just been terminated: it was to be reasonably expected that that event would prove favourable for the commerce and prosperity of the kingdom. The following year exhibited a new and unlooked-for event in Edinburgh—the failure of one of its established banking-houses. The family of Fairholme had for some generations been considered as of distinguished credit and reputation. They dealt largely in corn like their neighbours, in receiving money on deposit, and in exchanges. The partners at that time were Adam and Thomas Fairholme, brothers, which was also the firm of the house. In the course of the year 1761, in the prospect of peace, Adam Fairholme had gone to London and had speculated largely in the public funds, which, on an expectation of the peace taking place sooner than actually happened, had risen considerably, so that Messrs Fairholme thought they had acquired great wealth by their speculation, and indeed the general belief among Scotch people in London was that Adam Fairholme might have realised not less than £70,000 at one period. By his continuing his operations, they lost their imaginary profits; and being tempted like losing gamesters to enter still more deeply into the Alley, the whole affair ended most unhappily. Adam Fairholme remained in London, carrying on this scheme of stock-jobbing, probably with various success, till he was able to go on no longer, and in the month of March 1764, he declared himself bankrupt and left the kingdom.* The necessary effect of this was the bankruptcy of their house at Edinburgh, which stopped payment the same month.

As the misfortune of the Messrs Fairholme was known to have been occasioned by their speculations in the Alley, it produced no injurious effect on the credit of the other established banking-houses in Edinburgh. Nevertheless, the situation of money transactions there was extremely unpleasant. The rate of exchange for bills on London was as high as three, four, and even five per cent. against Scotland. This of necessity occasioned demands on the banks at Edinburgh for specie, which they were unable or unwilling to answer; and for that reason they avoided advancing money for the accommodation of the trade of the country, lest their notes, as would have infallibly happened, should instantly return on them for specie. In London the character and credit of Scottish paper was at the lowest ebb, and the Bank of England

---

* His fate at last was a tragical one. When in the vessel in which he had embarked for France, a Bow Street officer came alongside in search of a culprit who had made his escape from justice, and poor Mr Fairholme, having unhappily conceived the idea that the officer was in search of him, threw himself overboard and was drowned.

was extremely shy of discounting bills drawn on London from
Edinburgh. It was therefore a task of no ordinary difficulty
to conduct the affairs of our two houses with safety. For the
house at London, being a mercantile concern, was almost entirely
dependent on discounts, whose credit therefore the house at
Edinburgh was bound, for their own sakes, to support, as the
slightest suspicion against that establishment must have proved
fatal to the other. Through this troubled state of things, however,
the partners by prudent management were fortunately able to
steer without damage. The utmost harmony prevailed among
themselves, and Messrs Coutts behaved to us with kindness and
cordiality, evincing themselves on every occasion the patrons and
protectors of our establishment.

In the month of September 1763, I went to Holland, ostensibly
for the purpose of settling an outstanding account with William
Strachan of Rotterdam, the former partner of Mr John Coutts;
but in truth, at the same time, from a strong desire on my part
of visiting the continent. After remaining some time at Rotterdam,
where I received the greatest civilities from Mr Crawford,
Mr Davidson, Mr Livingston, Mr Manson, and others, Scotch
merchants, and making the tour of Holland, I proceeded by
Antwerp and Brussels, through Flanders, to Paris, whence, after a
stay of a month, I returned to Rotterdam, in order to finish my
business, in which, however—although from no fault of mine—I
made but little progress. Thence I came back to London, and,
after a stay of a few weeks, returned to Edinburgh, having been
absent four months. In February 1764, Mr Hunter went up to
London, where he remained till June; and Mr Herries having
resolved on a visit to Spain, Mr Hunter returned to London in
September, and remained till the month of May 1765. On his
return to Edinburgh, it was with extreme concern I learned from
him that matters were by no means right with regard to Mr
Cochrane. It had been always understood that he was not a man
of much property; but it happened that he owed some money,
although not to a great extent, to persons in Scotland, of which he
had not acquainted his new partners. His creditors, seeing him
now established in a respectable concern, called for payment; and
his partners, for the sake of the credit of the house, found themselves
obliged to advance the means. This, however, was no very
serious matter, as the debts were not considerable; but it was
discovered in no long time that his residence in London was in no
respect expedient. Mr and Mrs Cochrane, as I have said, lived
in the house in Jeffrey's Square, where the counting-house was

kept, and it soon appeared that their expenses were beyond what they could afford. Mr Cochrane, too, being totally unacquainted with the business of such a house, was not only unable to give any assistance—a circumstance which might have been put up with, because it had been partly foreseen—but was in hazard of doing harm in the capacity of an acting partner. All these circumstances together, seemed to Mr Herries to render it very desirable that Mr and Mrs Cochrane should withdraw from London; and Mr Herries determined, when the expiration of the first term of three years of the contract should afford an opportunity to make such an alteration, with regard to Mr Cochrane, as seemed to be absolutely necessary for the preservation of the houses, as well as for Mr and Mrs Cochrane's own personal advantage. In this opinion, Mr Hunter cordially concurred with Mr Herries, and Mr Stephen and I were most reluctantly compelled to give our assent also to the measure: otherwise a breach among the partners must have inevitably taken place, which might have been productive of the most injurious consequences to us all. For Mr Herries and Mr Hunter were resolved, at all events, to separate themselves from Mr Cochrane, and I well knew that Mr Stephen and I were utterly incapable of carrying on the house by ourselves, even with all the patronage which Messrs Coutts could have given us. Notice was accordingly given to Mr Cochrane in terms of the contract, that the partnership with him was to be dissolved at the end of the first three years. This measure was highly resented by Messrs Coutts, as an affront offered to them in the person of their relation. Much correspondence, as well as personal application, ensued on the part of Messrs Coutts, with the view of getting Mr Cochrane continued in his former situation. But Mr Herries and Mr Hunter, who had repaired to London in the month of January 1766, remained immovable in their resolution. In order, if possible, to preserve friendship among us, it was at first proposed by some of the partners that Messrs Coutts should hold Mr Cochrane's share in trust for his use. But this Messrs Coutts refused, and would not hear of anything short of his remaining in his original situation. They also urged, as a reason for declining it, that it might hurt themselves as bankers by their being supposed to be partners in a mercantile company. Afterwards they seemed disposed to accede to the proposition, provided it could be kept secret; but so many difficulties occurred about carrying it into execution, that Mr Herries and Mr Hunter declined it in their turn, and instead of a share of the house, made offer of an annuity to Mr and Mrs Cochrane, which was at last assented to by Messrs Coutts, when they found they could not make a better of it, and the annuity was fixed at £200 per annum during the joint lives of Mr and Mrs Cochrane, and £100 to the survivor, which continued to be paid to their dying hour. The separation from Mr Cochrane took place in January 1766, and a new contract was signed by Mr Stephen, Mr Herries, Mr Hunter, and me. This unhappy quarrel with Messrs Coutts put a period to all friendly intercourse between them and us, and I may safely say that no incident of my life has ever given me half so much uneasiness; for I considered myself under strong ties of gratitude to Messrs Coutts, by whom I had been at first received into the house—a very singular favour—at a time when they stood in no need of a partner. I therefore considered myself as standing in a very different point of view from Mr Herries and Mr Hunter, who had come into the house on fair and equitable agreement, at a period when new partners were necessary, and who had been selected by Messrs Coutts as the most proper for the purpose. It was indeed true, as they said, that they merely exercised a power which the contract left them, of dissolving partnership for the general good. But they certainly departed from the agreement they had entered into of allowing Messrs Coutts to fill up the vacancy, for which they urged the absurdity of such a clause, and the provision they were willing to make for Mr and Mrs Cochrane. I was compelled, however, to go along with Mr Herries and Mr Hunter, from a consciousness of my not having it in my power to do anything else.

Notwithstanding, however, this separation from Mr Cochrane causing a breach of former cordiality between Messrs Coutts and the partners—Mr Stephen excepted, who was not considered as having taken any part in the matter—no other apparent consequence took place, except the omitting Mr Cochrane's name in the firm of the house at London, which was changed to that of Herries & Co. But all friendly intercourse in business instantly ceased: with Mr Herries—whom they considered, perhaps not without reason, as the prime mover—I believe it was never resumed, and I shall have occasion to mention some events which afterwards tended to widen the breach between him and them. With Mr Hunter, Mr James Coutts had much intercourse respecting the politics of Edinburgh, when he came down in autumn 1767 to renew his canvass for the representation of the city in parliament, in which Mr Hunter, being a member of the town-council and a most active canvasser, was a useful partisan. To me both the brothers expressed more cordiality, being sensible, I believe, that although I had joined with Mr Herries and Mr Hunter from a conviction of necessity as to Mr Cochrane's retiring from London, yet that I was disposed to have brought about that measure, if possible, in such a manner as might have preserved friendship between them and us. When I afterwards went to London in 1768—where I remained a twelvemonth on Mr Herries going again to Spain, and, indeed, as long as he lived—Mr James Coutts behaved to me with much civility, as Mr Thomas Coutts has also done ever since, although he shewed a marked proof of there being no cordiality between his house and ours, by his employing Messrs Mansfield & Co. as his correspondents in Edinburgh. He and I still occasionally exchange letters, however, when anything occurs in which I can be useful to him here; and even that slender degree of intercourse I feel some satisfaction in keeping up, from a grateful recollection of my original obligation to his family. But to return from this digression.

After the execution of the new contract in 1766, the two houses were carried on, as before, with harmony, at least among the partners themselves. Little new or extraordinary, as far as I recollect, occurred in the way of business in Edinburgh until the month of August 1769, when the banking-house of William Hogg and Son stopped payment. Old Mr Hogg had carried on business in Edinburgh for many years with some reputation. He was a man very strict in the observance of all the external forms of religion, and he had been justly commended for having made a voluntary suspension of his payments from an apprehension that his affairs were in disorder. Having somehow got these arranged, he had gone on again with increased reputation and credit. But being extremely confused in keeping his accounts, as well as inattentive to the credit of those whom he trusted, and having allowed himself to be wheedled into a connection with a projector to whom he advanced considerable sums of money for working a lead-mine which totally failed of success, his affairs had again become embarrassed. His character for integrity, however, enabled him to continue to do business as if he were a man of solid property, and in this he probably deceived himself as well as the world, from the confusion in which he kept his books. On the death of Mr Hogg, his son, Mr Thomas Hogg, continued to carry on the house under its original firm, until, being able to go on no longer, he came to a stoppage as stated above. He had some turn for literature and belles lettres, and I entertained the best opinion of his honour and integrity. The engagements of his house were not very extensive; yet a number of people, who had deposited cash in their hands, lost money by the failure, particularly a great many mercantile people in Shetland. They owed a few hundreds to our house, on which we received a dividend, but which was not paid, nor were the affairs of the bankruptcy finally wound up for more than twenty years after.

No general bad consequences followed this bankruptcy, and the concerns of our houses went on without interruption both at Edinburgh and London. At this last place Mr Herries—who had removed the counting-house from the original situation in Jeffrey's Square, in which Mr Cochrane resided, on the differences taking place between him and us, to a house in Oxford Court, Cannon Street—continued to be the chief acting partner. Mr Stephen almost always resided at Edinburgh, and either Mr Hunter or I was constantly present to give him our assistance, or rather indeed to take upon ourselves the sole direction; in which we were by no means free from difficulties, not with regard to the carrying on the business itself, for nothing could stand higher than the credit of the house and the character of the partners, but by reason of the state of health of our partner, Mr Stephen, and the situation of his private affairs. I have mentioned that Mr Stephen had been originally a tradesman on a rather limited scale. He had been afterwards a partner in the house of Stuart, Stephen, and Scott, wine-merchants, from which he was brought to be a partner with Messrs Coutts. Having had no stock at his outsetting in business, I suppose when he joined Messrs Coutts he was not worth anything. His share in the house was not great, and the corn-trade in which they dealt was subject to much fluctuation. When, therefore, our new copartnery commenced in 1763, Mr Stephen owed a considerable debt to the old partnership, which was included in the list of those debts left for account of Messrs Coutts. But as he had an allowance of £200 for keeping a table for entertaining the friends and correspondents of the house, as his wife was an admirable economist, and he himself a man of no personal expenses, his share of the profits of our house had enabled him to make a considerable reduction of this debt. Still, however, we could not but feel some uneasiness for the appearance it would have to the world if, after having separated from Mr Cochrane because he was living beyond his income, Mr Stephen, who was now advanced in years, should be found at his death to have been in a state of insolvency.

Another unpleasant circumstance had occurred. Sir Robert Herries and Mr Hunter had conceived an idea that, the business of underwriting being considered a profitable one in London, the credit of the house there gave us a right to embark in it with a prospect of advantage, a measure in which my unwillingness to oppose any scheme of theirs induced me to acquiesce, contrary, in some degree, to my own sentiments, which rendered me averse from any hazardous kind of business. Conscious as we were, however, that Mr Stephen was not possessed of any property, we conceived it to be folly to share the gains which we looked for from this underwriting business with one who was incapable of bearing his share of the loss, if such should be the ultimate issue of the concern. We therefore entered into a mutual agreement to carry on the underwriting business for our own separate account, without Mr Stephen's knowledge or participation; a measure extremely reprehensible among partners, and, indeed, in direct violation of one of the articles of our contract, by which all of us were debarred from engaging in any trade or concern separate from the general business of the house: an exception in the contract had been made in favour of Mr Herries, but merely as far as related to the concerns of his house in Spain. This led also to a concealment from Mr Stephen of the private correspondence between Mr Herries, Mr Hunter, and me, which, till then, we had always mutually communicated to each other. As his bodily strength decayed with increasing years, he began also to exhibit symptoms of mental debility, and, like all weak men, felt not only a jealousy of his being deemed a cipher in the counting-house, but a desire to exhibit himself as a man of business. In those days it was the custom for the merchants and bankers in Edinburgh, to assemble regularly every day at one o'clock at the Cross, where they transacted business with each other, and talked over the news of the day; and as there were among the merchants at that time—I speak of the period before 1772—several gentlemen of a literary turn, and possessed of considerable powers of conversation, we were joined by many who had no concern in the mercantile world, such as physicians and lawyers, who frequented the Cross nearly with as much regularity as the others for the sake of gossiping and amusement merely. Amidst this motley group did poor Mr Stephen insist on exhibiting himself daily, a walking spectre of mortality, hanging on his servant's arm, in a manner extremely distressing to us his partners, and to every friend who wished him well. All these circumstances combined to make it desirable for Mr Herries, Mr Hunter, and me, to arrange for his withdrawing from the copartnery, which we were fortunate enough to accomplish by means of his two sons-in-law, Mr Fall of Dunbar, and Mr Blair of Balthoyock, with whom we agreed that we should make him an allowance of £2400, one-half to be paid in money, and the other half by an annuity of £300 per annum during his life. The money did somewhat more than extinguish the debt he owed; and the annuity, with Mrs Stephen's turn for economy,* was perfectly sufficient in those days for their comfortable subsistence. The agreement was signed in August 1771. Mr Stephen died in September 1774.

By this arrangement the sole property of the two houses of Edinburgh and London became vested in Mr Herries, Mr Hunter, and me, and thus the last link was broken of the original connection between Messrs Coutts and us. But we still continued to retain the firm of John Coutts & Co., which Messrs Coutts had not desired to see relinquished.

According to the new contract for Edinburgh, each partner had one-third. But a fourth of the London house was ceded to Mr Herries's two brothers, Charles and William, who, after being bred to business in his house at Barcelona and admitted partners there, had come to reside with him in London, and to George Henderson, Mrs Herries's brother, who had been originally bred a writer at Edinburgh, but on his sister's marriage had become a protégé of Mr Herries, and had also been sent to Barcelona. These gentlemen were announced to the world as acting partners in the house at London; but it was understood among ourselves that they were to be relieved by us of any bad debts that might arise beyond the amount of their profits. Charles and William Herries were both of them very able men of business, perfectly acquainted with the commerce of Europe, and therefore extremely useful assistants in the business of the London house, in which they remained till the separation of the two houses.

Very soon after this arrangement with Mr Stephen, two important events took place, extremely memorable in the history of the house. I mean the commission from the Farmers-general of France for the purchase of tobacco in Scotland; and the erecting of the Banking Company in St James' Street, London. The great company in France, known by the name of the Farmers-general, from their having farmed the public taxes of that kingdom under the old government, enjoyed by consequence the exclusive privilege of importing tobacco into France, with which they were chiefly supplied from Scotland, the article being originally procured by the merchants of Glasgow from North America. At this time

* She was his second wife. Provost Coutts's sister, the mother of his children, had been long dead. Mrs Stephen was a very worthy woman, and uncommonly attentive to her husband and all his connections.

Messrs William Alexander and Sons, merchants in Edinburgh, were the correspondents of the Farmers-general, and enjoyed the lucrative commission of making their purchases of tobacco; but they had become dissatisfied with the manner in which Messrs Alexander transacted their business, so that they were not indisposed to make a change of their correspondents in this country. Mr Herries, in one of his journeys through France into Spain, had travelled in company with a gentleman somehow connected with the Farmers-general, and had continued to cultivate his acquaintance as he occasionally visited France; so that when the conduct of the Messrs Alexander in the execution of the orders of the Farmers-general had been disapproved of by them, Mr Herries procured an order from them for the purchase of two thousand hogsheads of tobacco at Glasgow, a commission which he executed so much to their satisfaction that he was appointed their sole agent in Scotland. As this lucrative commission had been procured solely by Herries's personal influence at Paris, it was thought no more than reasonable that, instead of his third share with Mr Hunter and me of the ordinary profits of the house at Edinburgh, he should have one-half of the commission on the purchases of tobacco. In consideration of which, however, he was to be at all the expense of his journeys to Paris, as well as of any presents or other outlay which he might be put to in preserving his influence with the Farmers-general.* The other half was thrown into the ordinary profits of the house.

I shall very soon have occasion to mention the manner in which the house was deprived of this valuable branch of business.

The other event I have alluded to was our forming a new establishment in London. In the year 1768—almost the whole of which year and a part of the next, I spent as a guest with Mr Herries in London, attending the counting-house—Mr Herries contrived a plan for supplying travellers with money on the continent, which, for its ingenuity, deserves special mention, and of which the success fully rewarded the merit of the invention during many years, until the present war in a manner put a stop to all continental travelling. As Mr Herries communicated to me not only the first idea, but every subsequent step of his plan till he brought it to a state of maturity, it is with pleasure I look back to the many pleasant evenings he and I spent together at his fireside discussing this plan. In the course of his own journeys on the

---

* I recollect to have heard him say, that, the daughter of a leading man of the number being married while he was at Paris, he made her a present of a set of dressing-plate.

continent, and in the transacting of business, he had remarked that travellers were not unfrequently exposed to inconvenience and disappointment while abroad, by having their letters of credit limited to particular places, while they might wish, perhaps, to change their route, but from which they were prevented until they wrote home to have their credits altered, and, perhaps, before those new credits reached them, they had again changed their plans and wished to follow a still different route. Mr Herries bethought him, therefore, of issuing what should serve as an universal letter of credit in the form of promissory-notes, which should be payable at all the principal places in Europe where travellers were likely to be. For this purpose it became necessary to establish correspondents in all those various places who would give money to the travellers for these promissory-notes, at the current exchange of the place on London, without any charge or deduction whatsoever. The convenience to the traveller of this device was obvious; and Mr Herries was to find his profit from the use of the money, which of course was to be paid to him on his issuing the notes, till they again came round to London, after having been paid by his agents abroad. Such was the plan, which, after a variety of changes and modifications, he ultimately fixed on, and of the success of which he was very confident. As he saw the propriety, indeed the necessity, of its being undertaken by men of greater credit and capital than the partners of the house by themselves could pretend to, he proposed that a few gentlemen of opulence should join with them and form themselves into a separate society for the purpose. In the prosecution of this idea, he resolved to submit the plan, in the first place, to Messrs Coutts, with whom he still maintained intercourse, although there was no cordiality between them. Messrs Coutts, however, returned the papers, saying the proposal did not suit them. He also made it known to several other respectable men of business, who all gave due praise to the ingenuity of the contrivance, but all, like Messrs Coutts, declined taking any concern in it except Mr (now Sir William) Pultney, who was Mr Herries's intimate friend. Not discouraged by these disappointments, and still very fond of his project, Mr Herries resolved to set it agoing by the house in London, in connection with one or two private friends; for it was attended with no risk to those concerned, should it not succeed, beyond the loss of their labour in establishing the necessary correspondence in the principal towns on the continent, which he was enabled to do by means of his friends, Messrs Hope of Amsterdam, whose commercial concerns were more extensively spread over Europe than those of any other mercantile house whatsoever. As it was deemed necessary, however, that the promissory-notes should be issued to travellers from a banker's house at the west end of the town, as being more convenient than the city for those men of rank and fortune who were most likely to make use of them, Messrs Coutts were asked whether they would choose to act as bankers to the concern, and give out the notes at their house, although they declined to be concerned as partners. To this they agreed, and the plan was set agoing accordingly, and an account opened with them, on which some money was deposited in common form. This was about the year 1770.

When Mr Herries came to Scotland, in summer 1771, he informed Mr Hunter and me that he had good reason to believe that, although Messrs Coutts had agreed to be the bankers of the concern, and said nothing, as indeed they could say nothing, against the credit of the partners, they spoke of the plan of the travelling notes in so indifferent a manner to those who called on them for information, as rather discouraged inquirers from availing themselves of the notes than otherwise. He also said he had reason to know that they had been making inquiry in Paris, in order to establish a similar scheme of their own. Whether he was correctly informed, I cannot tell; but he declared his firm opinion to be, that either the plan must be altogether abandoned, or we must open a house of our own, whence these notes might be issued. With the latter view, he proposed that his uncle, Mr Robert Herries, senior, should be requested to join in the scheme, and become the acting partner, for which he was deemed extremely well qualified, by having been formerly a merchant in Rotterdam, although he had retired from business and then lived on his estate in the country. He also stated that in contemplation of this plan, he had, before he left London, been looking about for a suitable house, and had seen one for sale in St James's Street, which would exactly answer the purpose.

On his stating this idea to Mr Hunter and me, we readily went into the measure, from our deference for Mr Herries's opinion. His uncle was sent for to Edinburgh, and a contract of copartnery was executed, whereby Mr Robert Herries, senior, Mr Herries himself, his brothers Charles and William, and George Henderson, Mr Hunter and I, Mr Pulteney, and Sir William Maxwell of Springkell, became partners in a society to be called the *London Exchange Banking Company*, for the purpose of issuing promissory-notes to travellers, payable on the continent, to commence on the 1st January 1772, at the house in St James's Street, which, on his return to London, Mr Herries immediately acquired for the purpose.

As the first offer of a concern in the scheme had been made to Messrs Coutts, and they had declined it, and as it was thought impossible to continue to issue the notes from their house, because it seemed not altogether a business to their liking, I confess it did not occur to me that I was doing anything improper towards Messrs Coutts by engaging in this new copartnery, and it was not till a few weeks after the house in St James's Street was opened, that it struck me that this new establishment, although primarily for the issuing of notes to travellers, was to be, to all intents and purposes, a banking-house—by consequence a rival to Messrs Coutts in their own line of business. Mr Herries, in his correspondence with us, urged the propriety of our soliciting our friends to patronise this new establishment. My answer was, that when we knew of persons meaning to go abroad, we should certainly ask them to take travelling notes; but that I was scrupulous of soliciting general business to the house, lest it might appear an attempt at interference in Messrs Coutts's business. This produced an answer from Mr Herries, avowing that he had no intention to decline any banking business which might accompany the transacting of the travellers' notes, and then it was that I became fully sensible of the real nature of the plan. The effect it produced on the mind of Messrs Coutts was very soon fully explained to me by our friend Mr Seton of Touch,* to whom I had written, requesting him to procure me an answer from Mr James Coutts to a proposition I had made for becoming tenant of his house in the President's Stairs, Parliament Close, where the counting-house was kept, which was occupied at that time by Mr Stephen, now about to remove from it. Mr Seton wrote to me that Mr Coutts seemed not altogether disposed to give me the use of this house, probably on account of our new establishment, which he considered as a direct invasion of his own, which we were bound by every principle of honour to keep clear of, from our establishment having been originally of Messrs Coutts's own formation. This led to a correspondence on the subject with Mr Seton, who was the friend of both parties, and which goes at considerable length into the history of our original connection with Messrs Coutts: the two following letters between Mr Herries and me will still more clearly shew our sentiments on the question. On the 17th January 1772, I

---

* [Hugh Smith, son of an eminent merchant in London, had married the heiress of Touch, and now bore the name and arms of that old family.]

wrote, in name of our firm, to Mr Herries. 'We observe what you say of our writing letters to our friends in favour of the office in St James's Street. We have constantly recommended their notes to travellers, as they came in our way, and it does not occur to us that there are at present any friends who could be useful with whom we have much influence. But if we had, we are not very clear how far we ought with propriety to carry our solicitations, lest we should be thought to set out on the footing of rivals to Messrs Coutts in their own branch of business. We think, after what has passed between us and Messrs Coutts about the issuing of exchange notes, we are fairly acquitted to the world and ourselves for endeavouring, by means of an office in St James's Street, to obtain a more extensive circulation to those notes, and we can likewise see no harm in accepting any common banking business which may come to that office in a secondary way in consequence of issuing exchange notes: but we submit it to you how far it would be thought ungenerous in us, during the continuance of our original contract, of which there remain three years, and after we have risen to a state of independence on the foundation of the two houses which they transferred to us— although we pay them a valuable allowance for that transfer— that we should employ the influence we have acquired to establish ourselves in their own branch of business, especially as they would, no doubt, have made it a restriction in our agreement with them at first, had they supposed we would embark in such an undertaking. If Messrs Coutts take offence at our having an office in St James's Street on any footing, they may very probably recall the firm, and, in that case, it will be yielded up to them. But we are not quite certain how far it would be proper to relinquish the firm of ourselves. Perhaps the world would consider such a step as a declaration of hostilities on our part, and they might accuse us of ingratitude for thus affecting to throw off all manner of correspondence or connection with Messrs Coutts, after we had answered our own purposes by the original agreement we made with them.'

To this letter, Mr Herries wrote the following answer in the name of the house at London:

'21st *January* 1772.

'We have yours of the 17th, and are sorry to observe that you seemed to have misunderstood the intention of the hint we gave you to take an opportunity of mentioning to any of your acquaintance that you are concerned in the new establishment in St James's

Street. You might be sure we could not mean to desire you to solicit [business], either by the partners or their friends. But there could be no harm, in our opinion, in making the thing known by this means either to friends or others, and this was all we aimed at, leaving it to speak for itself, and everybody to do as they please. It is in this way that we have mentioned it by cards not only to our friends, whom we thought most likely to be of service, but also to several of the nobility; and it is very indifferent to us into whose hands those cards may fall, as no fault will probably be found with them, unless by those who are disposed to find fault at all rates. We neither in those cards nor in the course of conversation busily publish our intentions, but endeavour, as modestly as possible, to shew what they really are, without attempting either to conceal them or cloak our money-banking business under the former plan of exchange notes. If we were so disposed, nobody would believe us, and think meanly of us for making use of any covered language, when the truth speaks for itself without our telling it. Sir Charles Asgill and some others, before there was any appearance of a counter, or anything of that kind, in St James's Street, and before we had let anything drop of our secondary views in that establishment, plainly asked us if such was not the intention of that house, and you may be sure we were above denying it. We thought at first that Messrs Coutts and the other bankers in general would have favoured our plan, while we steered clear of any connection in their business. But the reverse has been the case with them all; and we believe none of them have applied for our notes, but when expressly ordered by their customers so to do, and in this way we have issued more in proportion to indifferent banking-houses than to those appointed to receive our lodgments in the Strand, who did wrong to accept of our business unless they had been disposed to do our plan common justice. It is plain from what one of them mentioned, on our first telling them of the formation of the present Exchange Banking Company, that they either considered that company already on the footing of rivalship, or suspected what has since happened, although at that time far from our intention. It is above a twelvemonth since we were informed that, in order to be on a footing with our plan, they had agreed with a house at Paris to pay their letters of credit in the same way as our notes, charging a commission of one per cent.; and we have been since informed, from pretty good authority, that they had written to Paris for a clerk, as was supposed to assist them in furnishing credit to travellers. Whether they mean to adopt our plan altogether or not, we cannot say; but we have heard that two banking-houses have this in contemplation. But we shall be noways sorry if they both put it in practice, since we think such an attempt will do us more good than harm. As to what restriction they might have proposed to us nine years ago, had they then foreseen the present establishment in St James's Street, or as to our agreeing to such restriction, it is impossible now, at this distance of time, to say what our feelings might then have been. But certain it is, that none of us were taken into the succession of their houses merely *for God's sake*, and Mr Herries, in particular, is conscious to himself that his fortune and principles were at that time so independent as to have prevented him from submitting to any restrictions not to do business—even had he been ever so dependent—in a lawful and honest way in any part of the world. All they had a right in such a case to require of us was, not to solicit their customers; and for this no restriction was necessary, as none of us were disposed so to do (or to take them), unless they come of themselves, in which case we are under no obligation to refuse them. It is also our opinion, and has been so for some time past, that we ought to change the firm; for we have no doubt that they will, however unjustly, accuse us of making use of their own name to draw their London connections from them, should any of those connections perchance leave them and come to St James's Street.'

In consequence of my letter, Mr Herries also wrote to Mr Seton as follows:

'I have received a letter from Sir W. Forbes, in which he tells me that you had written him that we had been soliciting Messrs Coutts's best friends in the banking way, and that you had seen one of our letters to this purpose to Lord Strathmore. You must give me leave to say that there must be some mistake in this matter. For I am as certain as I can be of anything, that I never either wrote or signed such a letter to any person whatever, and I am equally sure that neither my uncle nor any of my brothers would do it without my knowledge. What I imagine has given rise to this mistake must have been the card Sir William points at in his answer to you. I cannot at this distance charge my memory with the precise contents of the card; but I desire my brothers to send you a copy of it along with the present letter, and on a second reading, I daresay, you will be satisfied, as I fully am, that it by no means bears the construction you had given it. At least, I am sure that everything bordering on solicitation was meant to be avoided in these cards, which, in justice to the others concerned in the Exchange Banking Company, as well as to ourselves, we thought ourselves bound to write, not only to make our intentions honestly and openly known as to the money banking business, but also to prevent those who may be possessed of plans with *the first address* * from going to the wrong place, from whence some had returned unsatisfied. But on further inquiry,† had afterwards come to the city for notice, and generously warned us of what happened. Several of those cards were written at the desire of some friend or other of those to whom they were addressed, and I confess to you that we availed ourselves of the opportunity to send some to others, perhaps to many, without being desired, purely to make the thing the more known. When Lord Bute was last abroad, we were informed of his having expressed great approbation of the plan, and after his return, he desired a friend of mine to tell me to call on him to explain it fully to him. I never did call, but thought the least I could do was to send him a corrected plan on one of the cards in question, and had you been in London at the time, I very probably would have addressed one to you also, without meaning harm to anybody. I feel that I have been ill-treated by certain gentlemen, but I am not singular in this; and as we are all above being hurt by it, any sort of resentment ought to be beneath us. I know how much you are our real friend, and that it will give you pleasure to learn that everything here is just as we ourselves could wish, for I am thanked and caressed at all hands by those to whom our gratitude is due. I can also add that the necessary measures are pursuing to render the office as permanent as it is lucrative and creditable.'

Whether Mr Seton ever made any reply to this letter, I know not. My correspondence with Mr Herries, however, will shew what my sentiments were from the beginning with regard to Messrs Coutts, although, unfortunately, I had not foreseen what the consequences might be of establishing the office in St James's Street. At the same time I confess that, on mature deliberation, I felt very sincere regret that any such thing should have happened; and had I foreseen all the consequences, when the plan of the Exchange Banking Company was first arranged, I should probably have declined to be concerned in it, though I have no room to believe that any opposition on my part could have had the smallest effect in preventing the plan from being carried into execution, especially by Mr Herries, whose favourite object it was. Indeed, as his

---

* Meaning to Messrs Coutts's bank.
† Unintelligible in the original manuscript.

letters shew, he considered himself at perfect liberty to establish any fair and open branch of business in any part of London, where he thought it might be attended with profit, and that he had not otherwise attempted to rival Messrs Coutts than merely by making his plan known, and leaving it to speak for itself. In these sentiments Mr Hunter most cordially concurred. But still I, for my part, could not help feeling on this occasion, as I did on our separation from Mr Cochrane, that I stood on very different ground with regard to Messrs Coutts from the other two; but I must do Mr Herries the justice to say that, on my expressing this sentiment pretty strongly to him, he very readily offered to allow me still to withdraw from the concern, if I chose. The offence was, however, by that time given to Messrs Coutts, and my then withdrawing, while it would not have put a stop to the new concern as to them, could scarcely have failed of producing some disagreeable results among ourselves. I therefore deemed it expedient to let things go on as they were begun.

In this manner the establishment in St James's Street had its origin, and I shall by and bye have occasion to speak of the manner in which Mr Hunter and I withdrew from that concern.

If there had been but little cordiality between Messrs Coutts and us since our separation from Mr Cochrane, it may easily be supposed that this new occurrence put an end to every prospect of a reconciliation. Finding Mr James Coutts not likely to give me possession of the house in the Parliament Close, Mr Hunter and I resolved to hire that on the first floor of the same stair belonging to Mr Hope, which, though too small to accommodate my family, was sufficiently large for the purpose of the counting-house, and our principal clerk, Mr Bartlet (afterwards our partner), resided in it, to take care of the premises. To this new counting-house we removed at Whitsunday 1772.

About this time the partners engaged in two speculations, both of which turned out unfortunately—which, however, I am glad to record, because they strongly illustrate a principle which I hold to be of the first importance, that a person who is in possession of a natural and valuable branch of business should never allow his time or his attention to be diverted to the prosecution of objects which he does not understand, and which are foreign from his proper line, for such speculations rarely come to any good.

I do not exactly recollect how the first of the adventures took place, because I was residing in London at the time when the project was undertaken ;* but either Mr Hunter, or Mr Guthrie the partner of Mr Arbuthnot—with both of whom Mr Hunter and I lived in the most intimate habits of friendship and society—had become acquainted with a Mr Fraser who had been manager of a small paper-mill belonging to Mr Adrian Watkins, who held the patents of king's printer and stationer. On Mr Watkins's death, and the patents passing into other hands, Mr Fraser had represented so strongly to Mr Guthrie and Mr Hunter the advantageous nature of the trade of making paper, that he persuaded them to embark in a scheme of building a paper-mill and establishing a manufacture of that article. He argued that Scotland never supplied itself with paper, either for writing or printing, but every year imported to a very considerable amount, all of which would be saved to the country, and at the same time a considerable profit accrue to the undertakers, as labour was much cheaper in Scotland than in England. Over-persuaded by Mr Fraser's arguments, they accordingly feued some acres of ground from the proprietor of Polton, on the river Esk, near Lasswade, seven miles from Edinburgh, on which they erected a very extensive paper-mill, consisting of five vats and everything to correspond, all on the most enlarged scale, at a great expense—indeed, much beyond the original idea formed by the partners, who were misled by Mr Fraser; and he perhaps erred from ignorance merely, for, having been employed in a small work only in Mr Watkins's time, he had no conception of the expense of one formed on such an enlarged scale as that at Polton. When the buildings were completed, an overseer was engaged in England to conduct the manufacture, and, he dying, a second was brought from England, who also died. Mr Fraser then stated that he considered himself to be so perfectly master of the business as to be able to conduct the manufacture alone, and to him was accordingly committed the sole charge of the business, of which the partners themselves were totally ignorant; nor had they either time or skill sufficiently to control his management. The consequence was, that the manufacture was conducted probably at too much expense, and the paper made proved to be of an inferior quality. At first it had been agreed that the mill should be erected by Mr Guthrie and Mr Hunter at their own expense, and that our house and Arbuthnot and Guthrie as a

* When I say that I was absent when Mr Hunter engaged in and set agoing this ill-fated adventure, I am far from meaning to charge him with having embarked the house in it without my knowledge or consent. I have no doubt that he had both; but I had such implicit confidence in his judgment, that I allowed him to proceed with the undertaking without interruption.

copartnery should jointly carry on the manufacture of paper. But afterwards, the whole expense of buildings and manufacture were taken on themselves by the two companies. The business was carried on for about three years without doing any good, till at length the bankruptcy of Arbuthnot and Guthrie in the famous year 1772 put an end to the concern, and left the whole loss on our shoulders. Mr Hunter had by that time also become fully sensible of the folly of the speculation, and we gladly availed ourselves of the above event as a reason for bringing it to a close. There was a large stock of paper on hand, which it became necessary to dispose of, and with this view a variety of methods was resorted to. Mr Fraser's incapacity for such a situation being but too fully proved, he was discharged, and his clerk, named Duffus, was employed to dispose of the stock on hand. Duffus entered into a traffic with booksellers, giving them paper for the purpose of printing books, of which he took a quantity in payment for the paper, and selling or exchanging these books with the trade as he best could. Part of the paper, which lay on hand till the American war, was consigned to New York, whence I recollect we received account-sales, accompanied with an expression sufficiently descriptive of the quality of the paper—'that the printers of the newspapers had bought some of it because they could not find any of a *better* quality, and the apothecaries had bought the rest, because they could not find any that was *worse*.'

Tired at length of such a traffic, we made an agreement with Mr John Hutton, the lessee of the Melville paper-mill, to take over the remaining paper, printed books, and outstanding debts, for a stipulated sum, which enabled us to close the account, and ascertain the loss. The buildings and machinery had been sold some time previously for less than a third of their original cost. Thus ended the concern of the Polton paper-mill company.

The other speculation I alluded to, as entered upon by Mr Hunter and me, was, if possible, still more indefensible, because more of a precarious nature; but fortunately it happened that the loss did not prove to be very extensive. It took place thus. When Mr Hunter was married to a niece of the Earl of Cassillis, he became, of course, much connected in friendship with that nobleman, on whose estate there was believed to be a lead-mine, which had been wrought, though with no success, a good many years before. Mr Hunter, wishing to oblige Lord Cassillis, who was anxious that a further trial of his mine should be made, mentioned the matter to Mr Alexander Sheriff, merchant in Leith, who had a concern in the lease of the Earl of Hopetoun's mines at Leadhills, and was supposed to be master of the subject. Mr Sheriff, a man of a speculative genius and sanguine temper, grasped at the idea of undertaking to work Lord Cassillis's mine, and it was agreed that the earl himself, Mr Hunter, Mr Herries, Mr Sheriff, and I, should enter into a copartnery for the purpose, but limiting the concern so strictly, that we were each of us to contribute only £30 to a joint-stock, for the purpose of making the trial, and an overseer, named Barker, was engaged to carry it on so far as to ascertain whether we might reasonably expect to hit upon a productive vein of lead-ore or not. After working about a twelvemonth, Mr Sheriff became bankrupt in the disastrous year 1772, and this event, fortunately, put a stop to the undertaking, before any more than the original subscribed sum was expended, which, therefore, was all the loss that each of us sustained. I say fortunately, not in allusion to the bankruptcy of poor Mr Sheriff, who was a very industrious, honest man, but for us, as there is no saying to what lengths we might have been led, for I regard mining as a very deep species of gambling, whereby there has probably been more lost upon the whole than gained.

The year 1772 will long be remembered in Scotland for the numerous bankruptcies which took place at Edinburgh in the month of June, and which may be said to have entirely changed the current of the business in our northern capital. I have formerly noticed the extensive speculations which were entered into by some Scotchmen for the purchase and cultivation of lands in the newly acquired West India Islands; as well as the spirit which took place about this time for improvements in agriculture at home.* Some of the houses which carried on the banking business in Edinburgh, having embarked in these speculations, required a larger capital than their own resources could command. To this must be added, the rage which then began to take place for building larger and more expensive houses, than had been customary in Edinburgh before the plan of the New Town was set on foot; and larger houses necessarily led to more extensive establishments, as to furniture, servants, and equipages. At the same time those projectors and improvers, flattering themselves with the prospect of the immense advantage to be derived from their speculations, launched out into a style of living up to their expected profits, as if they had already realised them. Such causes combined had induced those gentlemen to have recourse to the ruinous mode of raising money by a chain of bills on London; and when

* [This is an oversight of the author. No such notice occurs in the earlier part of his manuscript.]

the established banks declined to continue a system of which they began to be suspicious, the bank of Douglas, Heron, & Co., commonly known as the 'Ayr Bank,' was erected. But, instead of proving a cure to the evil, they, by their improvident and injudicious management, found themselves compelled to plunge into this kind of circulation still deeper than the others, although with a more solid foundation. The fictitious paper in the circle between Edinburgh and London had thus arisen to an astonishing height, and was falling into great and general disrepute in London, when the first check was given to it by the failure of the London banking-house of Neale, James, Fordyce, and Downe, which had been but recently established. Alexander Fordyce,* a native of Aberdeen, had gone to London, and become a clerk in a banking-house. Having acquired some knowledge of that business, he persuaded Mr Roffey, a brewer, and a man of some property, as well as Mr James and Mr Neale, to establish a banking-house, of which he was to be the principal acting partner. Not contented, however, with the regular profits of their trade, he indulged in speculative tendencies, by embarking deeply in the public funds, in which he was at first successful, and was believed to have acquired a large fortune. In consequence, he assumed a splendid style of living; had an elegant country-house at Roehampton, in the neighbourhood of London; went into parliament; and affected a profuse generosity in presents to his relations and connections in Scotland. To crown his good-fortune, he had the address to marry Lady Margaret Lindsay, a daughter of the Earl of Balcarras, a lady of great beauty and accomplishments, doubtless captivated by the splendour of his appearance and the reputation of his wealth. His speculations in Change Alley, however, were not always equally fortunate; and having large differences to pay, he unwarrantably employed for that purpose, without the knowledge of his partners, the funds deposited in the house by their customers. The moment that this became known to the other partners, they very honourably stopped payment, in order that they might do such justice to their creditors as was still in their power; but this bankruptcy set fire to the mine, which at once

---

* His father was —— Fordyce, a merchant in Aberdeen, who had acquired some money as lessee of the York Buildings Company's estate of Belhelvie. This gentleman had five sons, three of whom were literary characters of eminence. One of them, a professor in Marischal College, Aberdeen, was unfortunately lost in a vessel on the coast of Holland; Sir William was a celebrated physician in London; James was equally celebrated as a preacher; Alexander, the fourth, was he of whom I am now speaking; and Robert, the youngest, was a merchant in Aberdeen.

blew up the whole traffic of circulation that had been carrying on for a number of years. All those houses in London who had largely accepted bills drawn on them from Scotland—of which the sum total was to an astonishing amount*—finding it no longer possible to discount the remittances that had been made to them for their reimbursement, were instantly compelled to stop payment, and, by unavoidable consequence, the drawers in Edinburgh were compelled to do the same. It was on Monday the —— of June —emphatically called the *Black Monday*†—that Fordyce's house stopped payment. Another banking-house in London, of older standing and greater eminence, which, induced by the idea of perfect safety, and the temptation of a lucrative commission, had become the correspondent of the Ayr Bank, and had been drawn in to go under acceptance for that company to a very great extent, also found themselves under the necessity of suspending their payments for a time ; but they soon resumed, and are still a banking-house of eminence. So great was the alarm in London that day,‡ and such the discredit into which every Scotch house was thrown, that there was a violent run even on Mr Drummond's and Mr Coutts's banking-houses, although they were no way engaged in or connected with the chain of circulation from Scotland. The resources of these two capital houses, however, were so great, and they answered all demands with such readiness, that the run on them lasted only during that single day. On Thursday afternoon an express brought to Edinburgh the account of the failure of

* Douglas, Heron, & Co. alone had £100,000 of bills in circulation when they stopped payment, and the whole circulation was computed at £800,000.

† [According to a contemporary record, the failure of Neale, James, Fordyce, and Downe, took place on Wednesday the 10th of June 1772. The author ought probably to have written *Black Wednesday*.]

‡ ['Every day was ushered in with the disagreeable accounts of new failures, and by the 19th no fewer than ten capital houses had stopped. Words cannot describe the general consternation of the metropolis on the 22d. A universal bankruptcy was expected. The whole city was in an uproar, and many of the first families in tears. Every countenance appeared clouded, occasioned either by real distress, or by what they feared for their friends. * * The Messrs Adam, of the Adelphi Buildings in the Strand, being unfortunately involved by the failure of some capital houses, upwards of two thousand valuable artificers and workmen, supported by their undertakings in different parts of the kingdom, were thrown out of employment, and their families deprived of subsistence. The poor men had begun their work in the morning, before the melancholy news of their masters' misfortunes was communicated to them ; when informed of it, they came down from the walls in silence, and stood for some time in the street in a body; and at last went off one by one, with every mark of regret for the fate of their masters, whose business had supported them and their families for several years. However, to the great joy of every good man, the Messrs Adam resumed their works on the 26th.'—*Scots Magazine*, June 1772.]

Alexander Fordyce,* and of all the confusion that had ensued among the Scotch merchants connected with the circulation of bills, whose fate was easily foreseen, as well as the effect of it on the houses in Edinburgh engaged in the same ruinous mode of supporting their credit. As expected, the bank of Douglas, Heron, & Co.,† and the houses of Fordyce, Malcolm, & Co., Andrew Sinclair & Co., Arbuthnot and Guthrie, William Alexander and Sons, Johnstone and Smith, Gibson and Balfour, Anthony Ferguson, and William Hogg, junior, all stopped payment in the

* ['The accounts of the failure of Neale, James, Fordyce, and Downe, arrived at Edinburgh on Friday afternoon, June 12th, by a gentleman who posted from London in forty-three hours.'—*Scots Magazine*, June 1772.]

† [The editor has elsewhere given the following account of this bank: 'The personage in Marryat's novel of *Peter Simple* who believed that everything now happening had happened before, would have had a support to his notion in the history of Scotch banking. The Western Bank was prefigured eighty-five years ago by the bank of Douglas, Heron, & Co., of which the head-office was placed at Ayr. It had been set up in 1769 with £96,000, subscribed by about a hundred and forty individuals, mostly unacquainted with banking business. It made notes without limit, and to get them into circulation, was unusually liberal in discounting bills. No poor struggling tradesman or farmer was refused credit to help him on. Men who applied to get their difficulties resolved by credit with Douglas, Heron, & Co., came away astounded by the unwonted facility they had met with, and laughingly declaring that such a concern could not go on long. It was thought to be at once a good business for the bank and a useful thing for the country. Of course an artificial stimulus was given to trade and to expenditure, and for a time all seemed going on well. But in June 1772, the great banking failure of Mr Fordyce created a general panic. A run on Douglas, Heron, & Co. commenced, and in a few days they found it necessary to suspend payments in specie, and to propose instead making their notes carry interest. Then there were meetings of well-meaning but ignorant gentlemen to express confidence in the bank, and offer to continue taking its notes, exactly as there were in the case of the Western. Leading shareholders, including the Duke of Queensberry and the Duke of Buccleuch, went to the Bank of England to ask assistance, precisely as the Western directors went to the Edinburgh banks; but the Bank of England, having already Douglas, Heron, & Co.'s notes to the extent of £150,000, was indisposed to trust them any further. There was next—exactly as we have seen in the recent case—a burst of indignation from the embarrassed bank and its friends against the Bank of England, without a word of acknowledgment of the great sins of the embarrassed bank itself, or of the justice of the punishment it was now suffering. This lasted till, in the course of a few months, it was discovered that there was a hopeless gulf to be filled up; and Douglas, Heron, & Co. closed business a little after the end of their third year, leaving an amount of destruction in their wake such as Scotland had not experienced since the wreck of the Darien Expedition. It is said that a large proportion of the land of the county of Ayr changed hands in consequence. For the remainder of their lives, its shareholders were never done with paying; and we have been told that their families, in some instances, did not get their accounts satisfactorily closed till some time after the passing of the Reform Act, at the distance of upwards of sixty years from the calamity!']

course of a few days,* and the alarm in Edinburgh and the neighbourhood became very general.

Besides the Bank of Scotland, Royal Bank, and British Linen Company, which were established by public authority, the only private companies that continued solvent were Mansfield, Hunter, & Co., William Cuming and Sons, and our own. On Monday a very smart demand for money took place on us all, just as had happened the preceding week in London. This was a new and an unexpected circumstance, for nothing of the kind had occurred in consequence of the failure of Messrs Fairholme in 1764, or of Messrs Hogg and Son in 1769. But as neither our house nor any of those others had been engaged in the circulation carried on from Scotland, and were sufficiently provided with funds to answer promptly all the demands that were made on them, the panic abated after two o'clock on Monday, and the public confidence in their solidity was restored, and even increased by this proof of their having conducted their business on a rational and provident plan, and avoided those speculations and that mismanagement which had proved so fatal to their neighbours. Mr Herries, however, who conducted the business of our house in London, being

---

* It was much taken notice of *at the time* that, only a few days previous to these extensive bankruptcies, a total alteration had been made by an act of parliament on the bankrupt laws of Scotland. As the law stood previously, any creditor, laying an arrestment on the effects of his debtor, secured to himself the value of the property thus attached, to the exclusion of all the rest of the creditors, even although arrestments should immediately afterwards be laid on the same effects by any other creditor. By this means a debtor had it in his power to give a preference to any creditor whom he chose to favour, by informing him privately of the situation of his affairs, which enabled that creditor to secure himself by arrestment to the prejudice of all the rest. And, even without supposing anything unfair of that sort, whenever a person declared himself bankrupt, those creditors who were on the spot had it in their power to gain a preference before those creditors who lived at a distance. The Court of Session had attempted to remedy this abuse by an order of court in the year 1754, declaring that all arrestments laid within thirty days after the bankruptcy should be of equal force; but this order was only made for seven years, and at the end of that period was not renewed by the Court of Session, probably because they did not think they had the power to make so great an alteration on the common law by their own authority merely. The abolishing of this iniquitous system, and the procuring an act of parliament to be passed for an equal distribution of the effects of debtors among their creditors, was the work of Mr (now Sir) James Montgomery, at that time Lord Advocate for Scotland, and afterwards Lord Chief Baron of Exchequer. After consulting with the principal merchants of Edinburgh and Glasgow, an act of parliament was framed which received the royal assent in June 1772, and the salutary effects of it were very speedily proved, on occasion of the numerous bankruptcies which now took place. Had the old system been still in force, the expense and confusion arising from the multiplicity of arrestments and law proceedings must have been altogether inconceivable.

uncertain of what situation things might be in at Edinburgh, or what support and assistance we might stand in need of, thought it a prudent measure to hasten a visit which he had at any rate resolved to pay to Scotland about this time, and to bring down with him a sum of specie. He accordingly arrived in Edinburgh about the middle of the week, by which time the run on our house was over. The amount of specie which he brought was but inconsiderable—only between £2000 and £3000—yet this, being, as usual, magnified by common report into a mighty sum, was not without its use in fortifying the credit and increasing the confidence of the public in the stability of our house.

On this occasion Glasgow suffered less, and experienced fewer difficulties, than Edinburgh. For although many of the considerable merchants were put to inconvenience by the shock which commercial credit in general sustained, only one house, that of Simson, Baird, & Co., stopped payment. Previous to this event of the bankruptcies of June 1772, a sort of contest had taken place between the merchants of Glasgow and Mr Herries, as agent for the Farmers-general, about the price of tobacco. The merchants, believing that the Farmers-general could be nowhere else supplied, and must give the price they demanded, would not accept of what the French offered, which was somewhat less. When the scarcity of money, however, in consequence of these bankruptcies, came to be felt at Glasgow, the merchants began to relax a little, and Mr Herries, on the other hand, prevailed on the Farmers-general to make a small advance in their price, to increase the quantity of their order for purchase, and somewhat to shorten their date of payment. All three circumstances were very convenient for, and agreeable to, the merchants, so that at once Mr Herries and they came to an understanding, and he went from Edinburgh to Glasgow to regulate his purchases, in which journey I accompanied him. As we thus went on a very agreeable errand, we were received with open arms, and entertained in the most sumptuous manner by the merchants during the time that we remained there.

Although our house had always been on the most friendly footing with the unfortunate houses which had now failed; yet, having never been engaged with them in the business of their circulation on London, we had no other connection with their affairs than by being accidentally holders of a few of the drafts on London of Arbuthnot and Guthrie, and of Fordyce, Malcolm, & Co., so that our whole loss by the bankruptcies of the year 1772 was but a trifle.

Hitherto, notwithstanding our quarrel with Messrs Coutts, the firm of John Coutts & Co., by which the house was designated in 1763, had still continued to be used; but as Messrs Coutts had it in their power to require us to relinquish it when they pleased, it was thought better that we should do so of our own accord. We therefore changed it, at the 1st January 1773, to that of Sir W. Forbes, J. Hunter, & Co., by which name the house has ever since been carried on.

The cordiality which we had recently experienced from the Glasgow gentlemen did not long continue, and differences soon arose between them and us, originating from the following circumstance:—There were certain advantages in the unpacking, weighing, repacking, and delivery of their tobacco, which the merchants had been accustomed to enjoy, and which they insisted were perfectly fair, but which Mr Herries affirmed, on the other hand, were improper, and in consequence would not allow to be practised, demanding that the mode practised in the port of London, which was more favourable for the buyer, should be the rule followed at Glasgow. This occasioned much altercation between them and us, and Mr Hunter, who managed the department of the tobacco purchases, did not always take the best method of smoothing matters. In this Mr Herries and Mr Hunter, I am perfectly satisfied, thought themselves in the right, believing that they were merely protecting the interests of our constituents, the Farmers-general. But, nevertheless, it produced the disagreeable consequence of making us unpopular at Glasgow, and rendered the transaction of our business there more difficult than it otherwise would have been. It was not long before the whole business took a new and an unexpected turn. Early in the year 1774, a new struggle took place between Mr Herries and the merchants of Glasgow, who held at that time considerable quantities of tobacco on hand, about a small difference in the price between what he offered and what they demanded. Things continued in this situation till the beginning of the year 1775, when, instead of improving, they grew worse, owing to the disputes which had by that time begun to take place between Great Britain and the colonies of America, and which threatened to put a stop to all commercial intercourse between the two countries. The merchants instantly took the alarm, and began to rise in their demands. Mr (now Sir Robert) Herries,* who thought, as many others did at that

* In the month of February 1774, Mr Herries had procured the honour of knighthood, thinking it might give him additional consequence in the eyes of the Farmers-general.

time, that the dispute between the mother country and the colonies would be amicably adjusted, and that the prices of tobacco would ere long return to their former level, advised the Farmers-general to wait a little rather than yield to the increase demanded. All this while the Farmers-general continued by their correspondence to express themselves perfectly satisfied with Sir Robert's conduct, and seemed to repose in him the most implicit confidence. They had intrusted to him alone their whole commissions to a great amount for purchasing in Scotland; and they seemed determined to employ no other agent there. While he was carrying on the most friendly and confidential correspondence, not only with them but individually with Mr Paulze, their president, who was supposed to have the greatest weight at their board, Mr Samuel Martin of Whitehaven, who had formerly been employed in purchasing for the French, made his appearance at Glasgow in the end of February 1775, and shewed an ostensible commission from the Farmers-general for a large purchase, in consequence of which he concluded a bargain for six thousand hogsheads.

When Sir Robert was informed of this transaction, he replied that he was certain Mr Martin had no commission from France; that the purchase, therefore, had been made on speculation, and that not an ounce of that tobacco would go to France. On his being again assured that Mr Martin had actually shewn at Glasgow a commission to purchase, signed by Mr Paulze, the president, and seven of the Farmers-general, Sir Robert communicated to us the following very curious anecdote as the ground of his so confidently believing that Mr Martin had no authority for what he had done. It seems that a very short time before, on opening one of Mr Paulze's private letters, Sir Robert had found enclosed in it a letter from Paulze to Mr Martin, consisting of a few lines, in which the president informed Mr Martin that he had received his letter, offering his services to purchase tobacco for France, but which he must decline accepting, as the Farmers-general were determined not to employ any other agent than Sir Robert Herries. By the following post Paulze wrote to Sir Robert that he suspected he had folded up in the packet to him by mistake the letter to Mr Martin, but which Sir Robert might put in the fire without forwarding it, as Mr Paulze said he had written and despatched another letter to Mr Martin. No wonder, therefore, that Sir Robert was so very positive that Mr Martin was acting without authority. But, on its being stated to him that Mr Martin had actually shewn his commission, the date of which was specified, Sir Robert resolved to send his brother Charles over to Paris to learn the real truth of the matter. On the return of the latter, after remaining but a single day at Paris, Sir Robert was thunderstruck to learn that he had been completely deceived by Mr Paulze and the Farmers-general; that the commission to Mr Martin was real; and that his purchase of the six thousand hogsheads had been approved of. At their interview, Mr Paulze informed Mr Herries that, for some time past, he had become suspicious with regard to Sir Robert's management, who, he acknowledged, had ably served them during the first three years. But since that period they had entertained the belief that Sir Robert was engaged in speculations in tobacco on his own account—for which, to be sure, some transactions of Sir Robert's had given a colour—and that he had all the while been amusing the Farmers-general when advising them to be in no hurry to purchase, expecting that prices would go lower, but in fact with a view of disposing of his own purchases to them at an advanced price. That he had purposely redoubled his marks of confidence in Sir Robert by seeming to approve of his conduct, in order that he might not interfere with Mr Martin, to whose proposals they had listened, in order to obtain that tobacco which Sir Robert did not seem disposed to procure for them. He concluded by saying that Sir Robert's only chance of retaining the business of the Farmers-general, was by executing the orders of which he was still in possession on suitable terms.*

On hearing this detail from his brother, Sir Robert found himself most awkwardly situated. He saw that he had trusted too much to the strength of his influence with Mr Paulze, with whom he had carried on a close and confidential private correspondence, and whom he wished to interest in some private speculations for their joint account, by purchasing tobacco in America to be afterwards sold to France, which, however, never took effect. By this correspondence, I am well persuaded, Sir Robert did not think he was guilty of any breach of his duty as acting under a commission from the Farmers-general; but he certainly acted in that respect

* One of these marks of confidence was the fictitious letter to Mr Martin above mentioned, which Sir Robert had found as if it had slipped by accident into Paulze's private dispatch, and it was no wonder if he was the dupe of such a refined artifice. This circumstance of Mr Martin's commission from the Farmers-general, the reality of which Mr Hunter, on Sir Robert's confident assertions, had too warmly denied in conversation with Mr Ronald Crawfurd of Glasgow, had nearly occasioned a duel, Mr Crawfurd having sent Mr Hunter a challenge, which he accepted, and a meeting was appointed to take place between them in London. As the affair took air, our friend Mr Colin Dunlop of Glasgow wrote to me of it, on which I went to Glasgow and was fortunate enough to get the matter amicably accommodated.

not with his usual prudence and discretion. On the other hand, he had rendered himself extremely unpopular with the merchants of Glasgow, who accused him of acting towards them with more rigour, and endeavouring to lower their prices more than his duty to his constituents, as their factor, required. They also plainly accused him of wishing to deceive them by holding himself forth as solely possessed of the orders of the Farmers-general, with a view of beating down their market, at the very time that Mr Martin had actually a commission from them for a large purchase. Sir Robert, therefore, felt himself ill off at all hands, and it is scarcely possible to suppose any person's situation in trade, with upright intentions, more irksome and unpleasant than his was at that period.

By this time the news from America of the inflammatory disposition of the colonists, and the prospect of a rupture between the two countries, had made the holders of tobacco raise their prices, not only at Glasgow, but at London and the outports of England; so that Sir Robert, who was now anxious to make a still further purchase beyond what he had already secured, although without any explicit order from the Farmers-general, was obliged to give so very high terms for what he got, that the Farmers-general seemed not inclined to take the goods off his hands. Had they persisted in this resolution—which, however, they did not do—it would have been rather for the benefit of the house than otherwise, because tobaccos still continued to rise in price, and those which we held would have ultimately yielded a considerable profit.

Sir Robert soon after went over to Paris, and from conversation with Mr Paulze was induced to believe that he had succeeded completely in explaining his past conduct, so as to be reinstated in the favourable opinion of the Farmers-general; and, in fact, he still occasionally made purchases on their account for a couple of years after this fracas from the merchants in Britain, who were still possessed of considerable quantities of tobacco, which they had imported before the disputes with America had come to a crisis. At length the rencounter between the British troops and the Americans at Lexington, on 19th April 1775, which was the first bloodshed in the quarrel, and afterwards the battle of Bunker's Hill on the 17th June of that year, gave a commencement to the war, which terminated in the independency of America, since which time France has been supplied with tobacco from that country, without the intervention of Great Britain.

This dispute between Sir Robert and the Farmers-general may be said to have produced another and yet more important effect with regard to him and his partners, for it ultimately led to the separation of the two houses. In order to explain this, it is necessary to mention that it was the practice of the Farmers-general to make anticipated remittances to the house in London, which, therefore, had always a very considerable sum of their money in hand. This had induced Sir Robert, trusting to the permanency of the commission, to engage, for the sake of greater profit, in mercantile adventures of various sorts—brandies, hops, rice, tobacco, &c.—to an extent beyond what he would otherwise have done, instead of employing the money in discounts of bills, or India bonds, or navy or exchequer bills, which, while they bore a moderate interest in the meantime, could always be commanded on a short notice on an emergency.

When the displeasure of the Farmers-general took place, and it seemed by no means improbable that they would close the account entirely, it became a serious consideration how funds would be provided for the repayment of the balance to them, and how the depending speculations in trade could be supported without the facility which their remittances afforded. This consideration gave no small alarm to the partners at London, as well as to us at Edinburgh, although Sir Robert himself professed to be noway uneasy on that score, and as the Farmers-general continued to carry on their correspondence much as formerly, no actual inconvenience did happen.

So very disagreeable, however, had it been to Mr Hunter and me, to see the house at London in this manner departing from their original plan of commission business, and engaging in extensive mercantile speculations, that we thought it absolutely necessary to establish some rules for its future conduct; and for that purpose the present time seemed the most proper of any, when the contract of copartnery was about to be renewed. It had been fixed for twelve years from its commencement, on the 1st February 1763, and therefore it expired on the same day in 1775; but it had been agreed among the parties that the commencement of the new copartnery should be postponed for another year, at which time Sir Robert's brothers, Charles and William Herries, and his brother-in-law, George Henderson, who had hitherto only enjoyed a certain share of the profits of the house by virtue of the agreement of the year 1771, were to be declared partners to the world, and sign the new contract as such. In order to arrange the terms of the new contract with Sir Robert, Mr Hunter had gone to London, and in consequence of what he and I had previously agreed on, it was proposed that certain regulations should be inserted in it, or in by-laws, for the future conduct of the business of the London house. This produced a very unpleasant correspondence between Mr Hunter and me on the one hand, and Sir Robert on the other, whose pride was hurt by the idea of having rules prescribed to him by his junior partners, while he had hitherto been accustomed to have the principal, indeed I may say the sole, direction without control. The uneasiness, however, which we had suffered from the extensive engagements the London house had embarked in, on the expectation that the funds of the Farmers-general would be continued, and the chance that those funds might be speedily withdrawn, had made so deep an impression on our minds, that we steadily adhered to our purpose. Sir Robert, on the other hand, insisted that his past conduct had not been so devoid of prudence or deserving of censure as to require stricter stipulations than formerly. At length, when neither side seemed disposed to give up their opinion, Mr Hunter and I received a letter signed by Sir Robert, his brothers Charles and William, and Mr Henderson, the purport of which was that, as mutual confidence seemed to be withdrawn, and a contrariety of sentiments to have taken place, it would be best to separate our respective interests, with which view Sir Robert's brothers proposed to relinquish entirely to Mr Hunter and me the house at Edinburgh, while we, on the other hand, should relinquish to them the house at London. To this proposition we most readily acceded, and at the same time, wishing to make the house at Edinburgh our sole object thenceforward, we also relinquished to the other partners the share which we held in the banking-house in St James's Street, London.

In our reply to Sir Robert's letter, accepting of his proposal of a separation of the two houses of London and Edinburgh, and informing him of our intention to resign also our shares in the establishment in St James's Street, we requested him to communicate this to Mr Herries, senior, and Mr Hammersley, the two acting partners in the latter company; thinking it most delicate to leave Sir Robert to explain to these gentlemen the causes which had produced this resolution on our parts. Sir Robert, however, had merely informed them of the fact, without any explanation. This produced a letter to Mr Hunter and me from Mr Herries, senior, written in the most friendly style, expressing his surprise and regret at our resolution of withdrawing from the Exchange Banking Company, of the cause of which he seemed perfectly ignorant.

To this letter I wrote at considerable length, explaining our reasons for the measure; and as it gives a detail of our situation with Sir Robert Herries, written at the time it happened, I think a few excerpts from it may not be without interest.

'20th *September* 1775.

'DEAR SIR—Your very obliging letter of the 11th was forwarded to me to Aberdeenshire, whither I came lately for a little relaxation at this dead season of the year. This has occasioned some delay in replying to it, which I hope you will be kind enough to overlook.

'In a letter which Mr Hunter and I wrote to Sir Robert Herries the 10th ult., on receiving his ultimate resolution in regard to the two houses, we asked the favour of him to explain to you and Mr Hammersley the causes which had brought about a separation. But, as you say Sir Robert has been silent in regard to the reasons of disuniting the two houses at London and Edinburgh, I shall beg leave to recapitulate them to you and Mr Hammersley in as few words as possible.

'You are no strangers, I believe, to what passed in regard to the tobacco-commission in January and February last. The hazard there seemed to be of Sir Robert's losing the friendship and orders of the Farmers-general at that time, first led us to consider seriously what might be the consequences, in the way of business, should that event take place. On a careful retrospection, we were vexed to find that, by reposing too implicit a confidence in the permanency of the friendship of that great company, and allured by the temptation of a very large deposit from them, of which there was no reason before that time to doubt the continuance, the house at London had been tempted to go greater lengths in the way of commerce and speculation than the natural powers of the house could prudently admit of, or than we can now approve. Very fortunately for us, the Farmers-general made no change in their system of remittances—although it seems it was only carried by a single vote that they did not then at once shut up accounts with us—and the most of the engagements entered into have since been brought to a successful period. But the embarrassment we had been in, and the anxiety of mind we had all suffered, for fear of any disgrace on the credit of the house, led Mr Hunter and me earnestly to wish that such a system might be formed and adhered to, as should effectually save us from any such disagreeable contingency for the future. We considered that the two houses had yielded most comfortable profits for many years before we enjoyed the French commission, and we saw no reason to despair of a like success by a continuance of the same prudent management. We could not but regard the natural business of the two houses as more permanent, and therefore more worth attending to, though, perhaps, less lucrative in the meantime than the orders or the cash of the Farmers-general, which last we therefore proposed should never be employed in trade, or in any shape where it could not readily be commanded, if the French gentlemen should withdraw their friendship. But, above all, we had in view the nature of your establishment in St James's Street and of ours at Edinburgh. These, as banking-houses dependent on the good opinion of the public, could not but be greatly affected by appearances at Jeffrey's Square of dipping too deep in extensive engagements, to which the private fortunes of the partners could not be supposed in any degree equal. We were even assured, in the most friendly manner, by those who wished us well, that we were already in the mouths of the world on account of what had passed, and that the utmost caution was necessary for the future to preserve the credit which we had hitherto enjoyed. All these reasons moved us, when we were framing our new contract, to propose to Sir Robert a plan of operations for the future, founded on that part of past experience which had proved the basis of our present valuable natural business, as well as guided by what we could not but think had been in many respects a too extensive though profitable class of transactions. Sir Robert thought it improper that rules should be imposed on him by partners inferior in years, experience, and fortune. We most readily admit we are by no means his equals in any of these particulars. But where men are independent, I humbly conceive it to be the very essence of a copartnery, that each member may suggest whatever he thinks will be most conducive to the general good, provided he do it with temper and good breeding. As to the opinion of the others, the world might, no doubt, form ideas unfavourable to us without any just grounds. But as, from the nature of our business of bankers, we are almost entirely dependent on the regard and confidence of the public, it ought to be our duty to study and comply with the prejudices, whether well or ill founded, of those who are pleased to employ us. In the whole of the business we can safely say that we had his interest at heart along with our own, and we think we are warranted in the assertion when it is considered that the credit of the house at Edinburgh was at stake, in which he is equally interested with us. If the reputation of caution should be lost, which the partners had gained by a prudent attention to their staple business, the house at Edinburgh could not suffer in that respect without the house at London being at the same time most essentially injured by it, as the two were so intimately connected together.

'In regard to the house in St James's Street, I have ever considered that establishment as wisely planned, and give me leave to add, without any flattery to you and the other acting partners, as conducted with a degree of assiduity and attention that have already surmounted the great obstacles which were always foreseen and must constantly attend every plan of that kind. We had, therefore, every reason to be satisfied with our situation in regard to it. But when we found that our original connection in London was to come to a period, we naturally thought of confining our views solely to the business of Edinburgh. To that consideration we were contented to sacrifice the prospects of increasing advantage which on the best ground you may hope to reap from the Banking Company. I have endeavoured to give you a detail of what has passed with truth and sincerity. Through the whole of our correspondence with Sir Robert on this occasion, I have acted according to the best of my judgment; and on looking back on all that I have written or proposed to him, I am happy in not finding anything that I could wish to alter.'

Thus ended all connection of partnership between Sir Robert and us—a measure the wisdom of which, with regard to the house at Edinburgh, the event has fully justified. But, although a separation of interests had thus been resolved on, as we had hitherto lived in the utmost degree of friendship and intimacy, we were all equally desirous that the separation should take place with good humour and cordiality, which our mutual endeavours were successfully exerted to preserve throughout the whole of the transaction. The fundamental principles, indeed, whence the separation took its rise, prevented us from committing to the house in London our exchange correspondence, which we judged it expedient to confide to some banking-house of distinguished eminence; yet we resolved to throw every advantage which we properly could in the way of the house in the city, as well as of the banking-house in St James's Street, by such parts of our correspondence as we could with propriety put under their charge, and to which rule of conduct we have ever since adhered.

Mr Hunter and I, being thus left sole proprietors of the house at Edinburgh, judged it expedient to assume an associate to aid us in conducting the business, as well as to guard against the inconvenience that might arise in the event of either his or my death. And we were most fortunate in having at that time in the counting-house a person of great merit, Mr James Bartlet, a native of Aberdeen, who had been originally bred to business with Mr David Gregorie of Dunkirk. Mr Hunter and I had received him as a clerk, at the solicitation of our particular friend, and his relation, the late Dr Gregory.

In that situation he had been with us several years, during which period we had had the strongest proofs of his abilities and steadiness as a man of business, as well as of his good temper and agreeable manners as a gentleman. We had, therefore, no hesitation in assuming him as a partner, and the event fully justified our choice, for he proved himself not only an able associate in business, but an approved friend and most pleasant companion to the last hour of his life.

By our contract of copartnery, which was to commence the 1st January 1776, and to last nine years, the shares were fixed as follow: Sir William Forbes, 11; Mr Hunter, 11; Mr Bartlet, 2 —in all, 24 shares.

The partners, having now no object of business but that of the house at Edinburgh, devoted to it their whole time and attention. And the world seemed to give their approbation of the change that had taken place, and of the system we had adopted, by the increase of our business and the high degree of credit and estimation at which we arrived. These circumstances were the more flattering to us, because the nation was far from being in a state of tranquillity, either in a political or commercial point of view. Hostilities with America had actually taken place, with various success on the part of this country, until General Burgoyne's unprosperous campaign of 1777, and the fatal event of his army being obliged to lay down their arms, induced the French to engage in the war as allies of America, with a view of humbling the pride and diminishing the power of Great Britain. That event produced an almost instantaneous effect on the money transactions of Scotland. The French rescript, announcing their alliance with America, was delivered at St James's on the 24th April 1778; and from that day we began to experience a drain of the money lodged with us on deposit, week after week, and month after month, until November of that year.

By prudent management we had been able to collect our funds about us, so as always to be fully prepared for the continued demand, and from the month of November our deposits began again to swell until they were as high as ever. Convinced, however, of the necessity of having our funds as much as possible under our command and within our reach, in case of any emergency, we kept a considerable sum always invested in Navy bills, Exchequer bills, and Ordnance debentures, which, while they yielded better than common interest, were not subject to much fluctuation of value, and could always be converted into money on the shortest notice. We even went a step further, and ventured to invest some money in the public funds. We did this, however, very gradually, and merely when we found a larger sum in our hands than we could properly employ in discounting bills, or making advances to our correspondents at home. And in making this investment we were always scrupulously attentive to keep so considerable a sum employed in those floating securities I have mentioned, as we judged amply sufficient to answer for every occasion we might have for money, even on an emergency. The public funds were at this time at a low price,* and there was every probability, as had happened at the conclusion of former wars, that they would rise considerably in value on the return of peace. The fund which we considered the most desirable, was the stock of the Bank of England; because, by holding a considerable sum of it, we derived a certain degree of respectability at the bank, and we had the chance of some advance in the price of that stock from an increase of dividend, beyond its comparative value with other government securities. Such an investment, by merely affording employment for our surplus funds, we considered as by no means coming under the denomination of stock-jobbing, as we never purchased a single shilling's worth but for money actually paid down, nor even that, when we could otherwise employ the money with safety and prudence, in the way of our natural business at home. The event fully justified the wisdom of the system, the merit of which is justly due to Mr Hunter; for, soon after the close of the war,† we disposed of as much of the stock as replaced the money originally invested, and divided the rest among the partners, by which means each of us added considerably to our private fortunes.

Mr Hunter, too, by the successive deaths of four brothers of his wife, had succeeded to her paternal estate of considerable value in Galloway, on which occasion he assumed the name of Blair in addition to his own.

* [The three per cent. consols, which had been about 90 at the close of the year 1774, were in November 1778 so low as 63¾. Bank-stock, which at the former period was 144, had now sunk to 110.]

† [In January 1783, immediately after the peace, bank-stock had recovered to 122.]

On the death of Sir Lawrence Dundas in the year 1781, Mr Hunter Blair was elected member of parliament for the city of Edinburgh, for which he was re-elected in 1784; and on account of his spirited exertions for the improvement of the city, by the plan of the South Bridge, while he filled the office of Lord Provost, he was, in the year 1786, created a baronet of Great Britain. As an addition, also, to the respectability of our house, I had succeeded to the estate of Pitsligo by the death of the Honourable Mr Forbes, on the 30th August 1781.*

In 1778 an event happened in the counting-house which is worth recording on account of some circumstances attending it. We had, some time before, taken as an apprentice a lad of the name of Watt, son of a decent honest man, a merchant tailor. He went through the usual routine of the counting-house, and among other parts of his duty, he had been employed as one of the clerks who exchange the notes of the country banks. It is our practice, after the notes are brought from the banks, that two or three of the clerks are employed to arrange and pack them up, to be sent to the country; and as the lads are all together in one room when employed in this business, they are considered to be thus a check upon one another. Watt had gone on tolerably well in the general discharge of his duty, except that he was sometimes idle and absent, for which I had more than once reproved him; but we had no reason to suspect anything essentially wrong in his conduct. It afterwards appeared, however, that he had fallen into bad company, both male and female, which had led him into expenses, to which the slender pittance he received either from his father or from us was very inadequate, and to support these expenses he was tempted into dishonesty. At first he contrived merely to secrete a bank-note or two, which passed as a mistake in the hurry of making such large exchanges at the banks, which must sometimes happen even with the most careful. At length he was tempted to commit a theft of extraordinary magnitude. He had been employed as usual in this exchange business on a Monday, and next morning he did not make his appearance at the counting-house. On sending to his lodgings, we were told he had not been at home all night, and neither that day nor the next could we learn any tidings of him; still we had no suspicion of anything wrong until Thursday morning, when a clerk of Messrs

* [Sir William succeeded to this estate as grandson of the Honourable Mary Forbes, sister of Alexander Lord Forbes of Pitsligo, a venerable nobleman who had befriended the Prince in the affair of 1745, and after whose forfeiture his son, the Honourable John Forbes, had bought back part of the family property, being that which Sir William now inherited.]

Hunter & Co. arrived from Ayr, and informed us that the parcel of notes which had been taken up at the bank on Monday, and sent to Ayr the day following, on being opened, was found short of the sum it was said to contain by upwards of £1200, while the external bulk was made to appear adequate by the inside being filled up with waste paper. It instantly occurred to Messrs Hunter & Co. that we had been robbed by the clerk intrusted to make up the parcels, and in consequence they despatched one of their clerks to give us notice of the state in which the parcel had been found. Watt having disappeared immediately after the notes had been packed up, there seemed no room to doubt that it was he who had made off with the money. The first thing we did was to send round to the principal banking-houses to inquire whether he had been calling for gold, and we learned that he had gone to Messrs Mansfield & Co. on Monday evening and got a bill at sight for £1000 on their correspondents, Messrs Farquhar, Kinloch, and Son, which he had taken payable to an assumed name. We further learned that a young man, who answered to his description, had gone in the coach which set out for London early on Tuesday morning, and it thus seemed clear that he had gone to London and carried the property along with him. It was therefore resolved that our partner, Mr Bartlet, should go in search of him, and he accordingly set out at one o'clock on Thursday; and as the weather was fine, and the roads excellent at that season, he made such great despatch, notwithstanding his stopping at Newcastle for two hours to make inquiries, and again some time at York, that he performed the whole journey in little more than forty hours. He learned at York that the person who had come in the stage-coach from Edinburgh had stopped there all night on Wednesday, and had even gone to the play. This, to be sure, did not look very like one who was flying the country; but his person so well answered the description, that Mr Bartlet pushed on and arrived in London between six and seven o'clock on Saturday morning. He went directly to Sir John Fielding's office in Bow Street, where, on telling his errand, a couple of officers were appointed to assist him in his search. Their first movement was to Messrs Kinloch and Sons, before breakfast, to inquire regarding the bill of £1000, when they had the satisfaction of finding that it had not been presented for payment. As it was concluded that Watt would be there as soon as the usual hours of business arrived, the Bow Street officers took their station near the banking-house, and accordingly it so happened. For, immediately after breakfast, they perceived a stranger with a Scotch accent inquiring for Mr Kinloch's, whom they followed into the counting-house; and on his presenting the draft for payment, they instantly laid hold on him. On Mr Bartlet making his appearance, the lad, without hesitation, confessed the whole matter, and readily went along with Mr Bartlet and the officers to the inn at which the coach had stopped, and where he had slept the preceding night, where he shewed them his trunk in which was the remainder of the money, except some which he had spent by the way.

Having thus successfully executed his commission, Mr Bartlet thought of nothing but to set out on his return home, after paying the officers for their services,* which he did that afternoon, bringing the lad along with him, who seemed to consider the business as at an end, now that the property had been taken from him. He therefore shewed no reluctance at the thought of accompanying Mr Bartlet to Edinburgh, just as if nothing had happened. And, indeed, it is not possible to conceive a greater trait of Mr Bartlet's own simplicity of character than his performing the journey to Scotland with the lad, as he would have done with any ordinary fellow-traveller, except that he made him sleep in the same room with him during three nights that they were on the road; and Mr Bartlet confessed it never once entered his head that the lad might have robbed him of the money a second time, or at least might have made his escape, had he been so disposed. No such thought, however, appears to have entered the mind of either, for they arrived at Edinburgh together on Tuesday before dinner, Mr Bartlet bringing with him the first account of his own expedition, for he had outrun the common post. On Mr Bartlet's arrival, a warrant was procured, and Watt was committed to jail. It was at first our intention to have had him tried capitally for the robbery; but on consulting lawyers of eminence, we were informed that it was extremely doubtful whether it might not be deemed merely a breach of trust, for which a capital punishment could not be inflicted, and indeed, perhaps, no punishment at all. As a trial with such a result might have done more harm than good, after his lying some months in jail, we assented to a proposition of his father's for his liberation, he engaging to send him privately out of the kingdom, which was done accordingly. He went to Carolina, where he got into a counting-house as a clerk, and seemed to be doing very well, until happening to go to a billiard-

---

* Mr Bartlet gave a very lively description of these officers, who, he said, were a couple of such blackguard-looking fellows, and their conversation such, that he felt himself relieved when he got out of their company.

table, where he lost a large sum of money of his master's with which he had been intrusted, he finished his career with a pistol, when little more than twenty years of age. A sad memento to all young people to avoid dissipation and improper company.*

A little before the period I am speaking of, being fully sensible of the great merit of Mr Bartlet, Mr Hunter and I, of our own accord, entered into a supplementary contract with him, by which his interest in the house was increased, and from the 1st January 1779 the shares of the partners were declared to be : Sir William Forbes, 21 ; Mr Hunter, 21 ; Mr Bartlet, 6—in all, 48 shares.

Three years afterwards, we made a further change by the admission of my brother-in-law, Mr John Hay, as a partner.† In the year 1774, at my request, Sir Robert Herries had agreed that he should go to Spain, and serve an apprenticeship in his house at Barcelona, where he continued till spring 1776, when he returned to London, and was received by Sir Robert into his house in the city—from which by that time our separation had taken place— and where, as well as in the banking-house in St James's Street, he acted as a clerk till summer 1778, when he came to Edinburgh, and entered our counting-house also on the footing of a confidential clerk during three years. Having thus had ample experience of his abilities and merit as a man of business on whom we might repose the most implicit confidence, a new contract of copartnery was formed, to commence from 1st January 1782, in which Mr Hay was assumed a partner, and the shares stood as follow : Sir William Forbes, 19 ; Mr Hunter, Blair, 19 ; Mr Bartlet, 6 ; Mr Hay, 4—in all, 48 shares.

Mr Hay proved himself in every respect worthy of the situation in which he was placed ; but I owe it in justice to Mr Hunter Blair's memory to say that the first suggestion was his, out of compliment to me, to bring my brother-in-law into our counting-house, with a private understanding between us that he should be in due time received as a partner if, after experience, we should find him suitable to our purpose.

At the same period a new and very remarkable event took place in the business of the house, which has been productive of the most beneficial consequences. I mean our beginning, at the 1st January 1782, to issue circulating notes in the same manner

---

* After it was discovered that he had run away from us, his desk in the counting-house was opened, when we found evidence of other acts of dishonesty and misconduct on his part.

† [Mr John Hay was eldest son of Sir James Hay, of Smithfield, Bart., and succeeded to the title in 1810. He died in 1830, aged seventy-five.]

as the public banks of Edinburgh. To explain this, it is necessary
to go back to a period even more remote than my coming into the
counting-house, many years previous to which the house of
Provost Coutts had transacted their business with the Royal Bank
of Scotland, and the house had continued to do all their business
with that bank down to the time I am now speaking of, during
which long period the utmost cordiality had always prevailed
between them and us. At one time, indeed, when the Royal Bank
was engaged in a system of warfare with the banks of Glasgow,*
during the Seven Years' War, the directors had suspended a cash
account we had of £4000, because they supposed our house to be
in too intimate correspondence with the Ship Bank of Glasgow,
of which Mr Coutts's relation Mr Colin Dunlop had been one of
the founders, and was still a principal acting partner. The Royal
Bank, supposing that our house had a hand in draining gold from
them for the use of the Bank of Glasgow, withdrew this cash
credit, as they also did the cash accounts of Messrs Cuming and
Messrs Kinnear, who were the correspondents of the other two
banks at Glasgow. When, however, the Royal Bank became
sensible that this species of hostility which they carried on with the
Glasgow banks, tended to no good purpose, they gave it up; our
house's cash account was restored; and Mr John Coutts, who was
then alive, became a director of the Royal Bank. Of course,
while the house continued to transact their business with the
Royal Bank, all their payments were made in the paper of that
bank; and as our business increased, and larger sums of money
were lodged with us at interest, instead of our requiring the cash
credit of £4000, we opened a deposit account at the Royal Bank,
where we lodged a sum of £20,000, for which the bank allowed
us an interest of four per cent. Besides this, we had also a
separate account for our daily operations, on which there seldom
or never was a less balance due to us than £20,000 more, for
which we got no interest at all. So that, in fact, we might be
said to receive an interest from the bank of not more than two
per cent. Besides the advantage which the Royal Bank made
of these deposits during the American war, when government
securities of the least fluctuating nature yielded a very high
interest, they had all the benefit arising from our making payments
exclusively in their paper, so that I am sure we did not exaggerate
when we estimated that our business of one sort and another was
worth to them not less than £3000 per annum. The bank directors, however, with a jealous policy, began to consider us and the

* [For an account of this warfare, see p. 5, *note*.]

other private bankers in Edinburgh as a sort of rivals, whose operations they conceived to be facilitated by those accounts of deposit which they allowed us, and concluding that we should be under the necessity, for our own credit and comfort, to leave the money with them whether they allowed us any interest for it or no, they wrote to us on the 26th April 1781, that after the 1st July following, instead of allowing us interest at four per cent. on the account to be operated on daily, they would only allow three per cent., on the condition that it should lie twelve months certain; and they gave a similar notice to the other private bankers who kept accounts of deposit with them. This measure, which we could not but regard as ungenerous on their part, led us to consider in what manner we might contrive to render ourselves independent of them altogether. Looking, therefore, at the extent of our business and number of our connections, and feeling the consequence which we naturally derived from these circumstances, after consulting with a friend or two on whose judgment in difficult cases we were most accustomed to rely, we formed the bold resolution of issuing a few notes ourselves, of the nature of bank-notes, by way of experiment, for which we thought our credit and character in the world sufficiently established. In order that we might act on solid grounds and in conformity with what we conceived to be the true principles of the banking business, we resolved that we should not employ any agent either in Edinburgh or elsewhere for the purpose of pushing our notes into circulation; but would merely offer them instead of those of the Royal Bank as formerly, in all payments which we might have to make for our ordinary transactions in the counting-house, and, should any persons shew hesitation to take them, or express a desire rather to have the notes of the established banks, we were instantly to comply with their wishes in that respect. For this purpose we had provided an ample store, not only of gold and silver, but of the notes of these established banks, until we should see in what manner our new plan was likely to be viewed by the public. Finally, we resolved that we should not enter into hostility with any bank, but, as far as depended on us, would live on friendly terms with all the world, being ready, however, to defend ourselves if occasion so required. It was likewise a consideration of some weight with us, that, finding ourselves very ill accommodated in the house we occupied as a counting-house in the President's Stairs in the Parliament Close, we had purchased a waste area on the south side of the Parliament Close, in which we had erected a most commodious counting-house, well secured against the danger of thieves or housebreakers, and of most easy access for those who might be pleased to transact business with us.

Having fully weighed this important matter, we set to work to prepare those notes which we proposed to issue; an operation of more labour, and requiring more time, than any one not practically acquainted with the business could suppose, resolving to begin to send them abroad into the world on the 1st January 1782, at which period our new contract was to commence.* Previous to our doing so, however, we wrote on the 5th December to the Bank of Scotland, Royal Bank, and British Linen Company, to inform them of our intention of issuing notes of a guinea and £5 on the 1st January ensuing, expressing it to be our earnest wish to live on the most friendly terms with them, and proposing to take up such of our notes as might come into their hands in the course of business, once a week, as the country banks did, or oftener if they pleased. On the 7th December we received an answer from the Bank of Scotland and Royal Bank, informing us that they meant to receive our notes in payment, but that as the British Linen Company took up their notes every day, the two banks expected we would do the same, a rule to which we conformed without hesitation. In this manner was our plan set agoing without difficulty. Every person to whom the notes were presented, either by ourselves or others, received them in payment without the smallest hesitation, and, as we have invariably adhered to those principles which we originally laid down, their circulation has continued gradually, but steadily, to extend, till the amount of our notes has not only far exceeded our most sanguine expectations, but has been one cause of the great increase which has taken place in the original and fundamental branches of our business—the deposit of money with us at interest, and the negotiation of bills of exchange between Edinburgh and London, both of

---

* A whimsical circumstance took place in regard to the date we affixed to our notes, which deserves to be mentioned, because it had some temporary effect in regard to their circulation. When adjusting the form of the notes to be engraved, we fixed on the 1st July 1781 as the date which they were to bear, without particular reason for preferring that date, except that it was the day specified by the Royal Bank on which they were to shut our account, in case we did not agree to the conditions they had prescribed. As ill-luck would have it, the 1st July happened that year to fall on a Sunday, which did not occur to us at the time, nor indeed till some weeks after we had begun to issue the notes, when we were informed that many people scrupled to receive them in money transactions, as supposing them not to be valid because dated on a Sunday. The objection, whether legal or not, was worth attending to, and, as soon as it was pointed out to us, we caused a new plate to be engraved and had the notes dated 1st March 1782.

which branches have been enlarged to a most astonishing degree, while, on the other hand, those branches of our business have been the means of facilitating and extending the circulation of our notes; so that they have mutually acted and reacted on each other.

In this comfortable train of business we went on till the year 1787, when, a break in our contract being about to take place at the 1st January ensuing, Sir James Hunter Blair and I resolved to reward the long and faithful services of an old associate, Mr Lewis Hay, who had been in our counting-house for no less a period than one-and-thirty years, by advancing him to the rank of a partner.* His father had commanded a revenue cutter on the western coast of Scotland, and his family had been resident at Ayr, where Sir James and Lewis became acquainted at school. His father having been laid aside from the command of his cutter, on some malicious information as I have heard, brought his family to Leith, where he engaged in the wine-trade with Mr Robert Grant, nephew to our Mr Stephen. But Captain Hay being quite unacquainted with mercantile business, his partner and he could not agree, and of course separated. His eldest son, Lewis, became a clerk in the Custom-house of Leith, where he first acquired the habit of that correct and never-ceasing application to business which stuck by him to the latest period of his life. At the request of Mr Bell, wine-merchant in Leith, Lewis was received into our counting-house as a clerk, about a year after me. He had a brother, George, who engaged in the trade of making shoes for wholesale exportation, on the joint account of his brother and himself. In this business they were not successful, and, his brother dying soon after, the creditors, sensible that Lewis had made a fair surrender of the effects which belonged to the concern, accepted of such dividend as could be afforded, and left him undisturbed in the possession of the moderate salary which he earned in our house, and out of which he supported his father and mother. He was indeed a most meritorious character, correct in the discharge of all the relative duties of a man and a Christian, and he had proved himself most useful to us in the general superintendence of the business of the counting-house, from which he never was absent, almost for a moment. He was therefore well entitled to this mark of our favour; but, previous to such a con-

---

* I had been in the house about a year before Sir James and Mr Hay came to it. We were now what might be justly called the only original members of the counting-house; every other person whom we found there when we entered —master, clerk, and apprentice—having been long dead.

nection taking place, it became necessary that he should receive a regular discharge from his and his brother's creditors, for although they had given him no disturbance while he remained in the station of a clerk, they might not have been so indulgent when they should see him a partner in our house. As some part of what he had owed was to ourselves, this we discharged without hesitation, and a proposal was submitted to the rest of the creditors to make them a payment on giving him a discharge in full, to which they all most readily agreed.*

Before the contemplated break in our contract arrived, a most unexpected event took place, which overwhelmed us all with the deepest sorrow. It was the death of our worthy partner and most intimate friend, Sir James Hunter Blair. He had set out with Lady Blair in the end of April for Harrogate, where he proposed to drink the waters for a scorbutic complaint, which was sometimes troublesome to him. A few days after his arrival there, he went on some business to London, where he remained only four days, after which he returned to Harrogate. Their children at home having been seized with the hooping-cough, Lady Blair came down to Edinburgh by herself to attend them, leaving Sir James to drink the waters. I continued frequently to receive letters from him down to the 20th June, on which day he wrote to me that he proposed to leave Harrogate on the 27th, to be at Newcastle the 28th, and at Dunbar the 29th. But how vain are all our projects! and so true is the observation of the poet, that

> 'On our firmest resolutions
> The silent and inaudible foot of death
> Steals like a thief;'

for while I was in the full expectation of seeing him return as he proposed, Mr Hamilton of Wishaw arrived from Harrogate on the morning of the 30th June, and told me that Sir James had been seized a few days before with a fever, which had made such rapid progress, that on the 28th, when he (Mr Hamilton) had left Harrogate, his life was despaired of. On communicating this intelligence to Lady Blair, but without saying how dangerously ill he was, she set out in a couple of hours, attended by a maid-servant and Dr Gregory; Mr Wood, the family surgeon, followed them next morning. It was, however, all in vain; for by the time Lady

* [Mr Lewis Hay, subsequently to this period, married Miss Margaret Chalmers, daughter of Mr James Chalmers of Fingland, and noted in our literary history as the friend and correspondent of Robert Burns, over whose mind her virtues and intelligence enabled her to exercise a considerable influence.]

Blair reached Northallerton, she was met by an express with the news of her dear husband's death, which happened on the 1st of July 1787, in the forty-sixth year of his age.*

The loss of Sir James Hunter Blair was a most severe misfortune to his family, to his partners, and to the city of Edinburgh. His family, consisting of three sons and three daughters, were all young, his eldest son being only fifteen years of age; a fourth son was added after his death. We, his partners, were deprived of a most able associate in business. Edinburgh lost by his death a most active magistrate, who had projected and carried on public works equally conducive to the ornament and advantage of the city. I, in particular, was deprived by his death of a friend whom I can never replace, with whom I had lived in a degree of intimacy which few brothers can boast of during one-and-thirty years, in which long period we never had a difference nor a separation of interest. It has been stated how we went on together from the time of our apprenticeship, till we gradually arrived, after a variety of changes, to be at the head of the house. But I should do great injustice to his superior talents, did I not declare that to him it was chiefly owing that the house rose to such a pitch of unlooked-for prosperity and reputation. He possessed a sound and manly understanding and an excellent heart. In his friendships he was warm, steady, and sincere, and ever ready to promote the interest of those to whom he formed an attachment. In his disposition he was cheerful and fond of society, and his house was at all times distinguished for hospitality. As a magistrate, he was active and zealous in the discharge of his duty; as a senator, he was honestly independent, supporting the measures of the ministers of the crown when he thought them consistent with the principles of the constitution and the good of the people. Too early and too deeply immersed in business, he had little or no leisure for study, and was therefore but little acquainted with books or literature; but he possessed, in an eminent degree, a species of knowledge of the utmost importance to him as a man of business—great knowledge of the world, and an almost intuitive discernment of the characters of men. In business, both of a public and private nature, he was skilful and active, and capable of the most unwearied application, and his plans in general were contrived with prudence and executed with steadiness. Of this a memorable proof was afforded by the magnificent idea, which he

* [Burns, who, partly on account of his Ayr nativity, had been treated with much kindness by Sir James, gave vent to his feelings on this occasion by an elegy, which will be found in his works.]

formed on his being elected Lord Provost of Edinburgh, of a communication between the High Street and the south side of the city, by a bridge over the Cowgate. In the prosecution of which extensive and important improvement, notwithstanding he met with no inconsiderable degree of opposition from ignorant and interested individuals, he was not to be discouraged, but kept on the even tenor of his way, combating the prejudices of some and the influence of others, till at last he accomplished his purpose. In his temper there was a degree of warmth, which, in the pursuit of a favourite object, or in the heat of an argument, occasionally bordered on vehemence and impetuosity, and which sometimes, in the intercourse of society, led him to forget or overlook what Lord Chesterfield calls the graces. In his notions of right and wrong, he was rigid and even stern, and he had no allowance to make where he perceived in others any departure from the standard he had formed of propriety of conduct. But his virtues will be remembered and the utility of his public conduct felt and applauded long after those slight imperfections are consigned to oblivion.

A few days before I received the account of Sir James's illness, and when, God knows! I had little notion which of us was first to pay the debt of nature, I had written to him about a plan that had occurred to me for continuing an interest in our house to the eldest son of any of the partners who should happen to die. It had often been a subject of conversation between him and me, how hard it would be, were either of us to die, that our family should entirely lose the benefit of their father's exertions in having brought the house into such a respectable position, and we had several years before entered into a mutual agreement, that whichever of us should survive the other, should pay to the son of the deceased an annuity of £500 a-year during eight years. But even this I did not think enough, and therefore proposed that the son should be entitled, if he chose, to an interest in the house of one-third of his father's share, which the surviving partners were to hold for his account until the termination of the contract, but without the son being permitted to interfere in the management of the business. This letter Sir James had received, but had not had time to answer before he was seized with his last illness. It was found among his papers after his death, and as it contained the strongest proof I could give of my belief in the utility of the proposal, I was anxious that it should still be acted on; and therefore, with the concurrence of the other partners, I proposed to the tutors to whom Sir James had left the care of his family, that a new contract should be entered into on that footing. Of this plan the tutors gave their most cordial approbation; but a difficulty occurred which seemed to present an insuperable bar to its taking effect. Had Sir James lived to execute our new contract, he could of course have bound his son and successor to any conditions he pleased. But his eldest son, being left a minor, could not engage in any contract or become bound to the world for his proportional share of the engagements of the house. In order to get the better of this difficulty, the tutors,* being impressed with the importance of preserving an interest in the house to their young ward, were pleased to carry their approbation so far as, with an unexampled confidence in us, the other partners, to take upon themselves the responsibility, and to become personally bound for young Sir John Blair until he should come of age and confirm the contract himself—a measure which reflected the highest honour as well on them who conferred, as on us who received, such a proof of their confidence. In conformity with this arrangement, a new contract was executed for twelve years from 1st January 1788, the shares being thus divided—Sir William Forbes, 16; James Bartlet, 7; John Hay, 7; Lewis Hay, 2; Sir John Blair, $5\frac{1}{3}$; the remaining of Sir James's shares, $10\frac{2}{3}$, being kept unappropriated, in case any desirable partner should come in our way. In the meantime, the profit belonging to those shares undisposed of went to the other partners in proportion to their respective interests in the house. Scarcely had this contract commenced, when we experienced another severe domestic misfortune by the death of our worthy partner and friend Mr Bartlet, whose talents as a man of business, and his application to the management of our affairs, had rendered him highly useful to us. For some time Mr Bartlet had been afflicted with a violent pain in the elbow-joint of his right arm, which had disabled him from writing or attending the counting-house since November 1786. At last the complaint had increased to such a degree that the surgeons who attended him, and who were of course the most skilful in Edinburgh, declared that amputation of his arm was the only chance left for saving his life; an operation to which he submitted with great fortitude in May 1787, and his recovery had proceeded so well as to give us the greatest hopes, that although he might not be able to take the same laborious share in the executive business as formerly, he would still continue a most valuable associate on whose knowledge of business and sound

---

* They were Lady Blair, the Earl of Cassillis, Mr Kennedy of Dunure, Dr Gregory, Mr John Buchan, writer to the Signet, and myself.

judgment we might with confidence rely. His constitution, however, was now so much shattered by his long confinement and suffering, that he was advised to pass the winter in a warm climate, in order to perfect his recovery. In this expedition he was to be accompanied by Dr Cairnie, an intimate friend of ours, and who had made a sort of employment of attending invalids abroad, for which he was eminently qualified by his medical skill and humane disposition, as well as by his acquaintance with foreign countries. They accordingly set out in September 1787 for Marseilles, where Mr Bartlet proposed to fix his residence for the winter.

Finding, however, after passing some weeks there, that, instead of making any progress in recovery, his strength was daily decaying, he was seized with an anxiety to return home. For which purpose he hired a vessel at Marseilles, on which, in the end of November, he embarked for Scotland, leaving Dr Cairnie, who had an insuperable aversion to the sea, to return by land. The passage was exceedingly stormy, and it was long before we received any tidings of his voyage. Our first and indeed only letter was from Gibraltar, where the vessel had touched. After leaving which, and just when he had got within sight of land on the north-west coast of Ireland, he sunk under his indisposition on the 9th February 1788, sincerely lamented by his partners and a numerous circle of acquaintance.

Mr Bartlet was characterised by a most excellent disposition, a warm and friendly heart, a sound judgment, and the most gentle and obliging manners. These qualifications he had improved by reading and intercourse with the world. He was a cheerful and most agreeable companion, and at the same time indefatigable in business, of which he was perfectly master. His death, therefore, we could not but regard as a heavy misfortune, not only as the loss of an able assistant in the counting-house, but of a friend for whom we entertained the most sincere regard and esteem.

Sir James Blair had intended to send his eldest son to France for a twelvemonth for his education, and he had even engaged a lodging for him in Paris. Sir James's death, however, made some change in that respect absolutely necessary; for the guardians of young Sir John did not think it expedient to send him to live at Paris by himself, now that his father was dead, and when, of course, he would soon be possessed of high notions of his own fortune and consequence. We therefore resolved that he should be accompanied by some proper person for directing his studies and superintending his conduct, and Mr Arbuthnot, junior, was engaged for this purpose. In like manner I had formed the plan of sending to France my eldest son, William, who was a year older than Sir John Blair, and I had determined, on the recommendation of Sir Robert Herries, to fix his residence at Lyons, in the house of a Swiss Protestant clergyman, who proposed to undertake the tuition of half-a-dozen young gentlemen. Mr Bartlet's going abroad seemed a good opportunity for their all going together, and they set out accordingly for Paris, where Sir John and Mr Arbuthnot left them. My son continued the journey to Lyons, where Dr Cairnie and Mr Bartlet put him into Mr Trossart's hands. I soon found, however, that his house was by no means an eligible situation; for Sir Robert Herries, in his zeal to serve Mr Trossart, had recommended his house to several others of his friends, so that almost all his pupils were English: by consequence my principal object of sending William to France to acquire the language, was entirely defeated, as it was scarcely to be expected that half-a-dozen lads living together in the same house could avoid almost constantly speaking their own language.

I therefore resolved, after William had remained there about six months, to send him to Paris, where, by means of my friend Mr Livingston, who happened to be there, I got him placed in the *Collége de Montagu*, in the house of a Professor Bouily, where he had not only the benefit of general study under the direction of the professor, but also the best opportunity of acquiring French, as neither the professor himself, nor any one within the walls of the college, spoke anything else. There he remained six months more, till I thought he had sufficiently accomplished the purpose of my sending him abroad.

Almost immediately on the commencement of our new contract, and before we received accounts of Mr Bartlet's death, two events took place, which rendered that year not a little remarkable in the history of our house—I mean the bankruptcy, first of Charles and Robert Fall of Dunbar, and, a few weeks afterwards, of James Stein and John Stein, with all of whom we were in the course of extensive transactions.

Charles and Robert Fall carried on business in corn on a very large scale, among the largest indeed in Scotland. James Fall, the father of Robert, and founder of the house, was a merchant of considerable eminence; so much so, that he had been member of parliament for the district of burghs, of which his native town of Dunbar was one, and in which he had always retained the chief political influence. Charles was his nephew, but Robert was the principal acting partner in the house after his father's death, and between him and Messrs Coutts there had not only been a great deal of commercial correspondence in reference to the corn trade,* but also much intercourse of personal friendship, which had been strongly cemented by the marriage of Mr Robert Fall with our partner Mr Stephen's eldest daughter. Charles Fall died, and although the firm was still continued, the business was thenceforth solely in the person of Robert. This correspondence between Mr Fall's house and ours had subsisted for upwards of forty years, during which their operations had been considerable, and the advances of money made to them were proportionately large, but always on the footing of being covered by deposits of bills and other securities. For a considerable time, however, Mr Fall had begun to shew an appearance of being in want of money. He was less punctual in his remittances, and these were frequently short of what they ought to have been. This naturally created some suspicion in our minds that he was not in a prosperous situation; for it may be laid down as an infallible axiom in business, that although any man may at a particular time be in want of money from some unforeseen disappointment or other, which it will be his endeavour as soon as possible to remedy, yet the merchant who appears to be constantly in a state of difficulty, is either unsound at bottom, or he is carrying on business more extensive than his own capital is equal to. And in either of these cases his correspondence is carefully to be avoided. This seemed evidently to be the case with Mr Fall. As we knew, however, that he possessed property both in land and houses at Dunbar, part of which he retained for political purposes in connection with that burgh, we considered that property as a sort of guarantee for the safety of his operations with our house. Still, we endeavoured to be as guarded with him as possible, frequently remonstrating against the irregularity of his remittances, and endeavouring to keep ourselves well covered. Yet, being somewhat suspicious that he was not in a prosperous state before Sir James Hunter Blair went to Harrogate, he and I had written a strenuous remonstrance to him in our joint names, as private friends, insisting, for his own sake as well as ours, that he would lay before us a state of his affairs. In answer to this earnest application, Mr Fall sent us a statement of his landed property, and a balance sheet of his books, from which we were led to believe that, although he did not seem to be opulent, yet upon the whole he might be reckoned more than equal with the world. After Sir James's

* Mr Fall had also introduced into Scotland the curing of red herrings, and he had chiefly brought about the formation of the East Lothian and Merse whale-fishing company stationed at Dunbar.

death, however, we became still more anxious to have his account brought into regular order, yet were very unwilling to take any strong steps for that purpose, with a house who had been so many years in close correspondence with our predecessors. In this manner things went on during the remainder of the year 1787, till at last Mr Fall, being disappointed of assistance which he expected from some of his friends, found he could go on no longer, and in January 1788 was compelled to stop payment. The balance which he owed us on account was no less than £17,000; but as we held a number of bills remitted to us in the course of our correspondence, we did not apprehend that we should be any considerable losers in the long-run. Trusting to that circumstance, we, very incautiously as well as needlessly, allowed our names to be used for a sequestration of his effects under the bankrupt law, and proved our debt to its full extent. It being thus published to the world that Mr Fall was so deeply indebted to us, some alarm arose, particularly among the farmers of East Lothian and Berwickshire, who had money lodged with us, and among whom Mr Fall's bankruptcy made much noise, and for a few days it occasioned some run on our house for money. But it was confined to the lower ranks, and soon ceased. Our ultimate loss by this bankruptcy, although more than we had laid our account with at the time when it happened, was but inconsiderable.

Scarcely had this alarm subsided, when other bankruptcies took place, which at first threatened the most serious consequences. James Stein at Kilbagie, and John Stein at Kennetpans, both in the neighbourhood of Alloa, two brothers, had carried on the business of distilling of malt spirits to an extent hitherto unknown in Scotland. They were correspondents of our house, and their transactions, particularly James's, were to a very large amount. Not content with the sale of spirits in Scotland, they resolved to rival the distillers of London by manufacturing spirits for the English market, which they conceived themselves enabled to do by some advantages in their situation in Scotland, where fuel and labour were cheaper than in London. They therefore hired warehouses in London, and sent very large quantities of spirits to that market, consigned to a house under the firm of Sandeman and Graham, whose sole occupation was the acting as their agents. As they were known to have made money at one period, and as they preserved the utmost punctuality and regularity in all their transactions, they arrived at a considerable degree of credit. In this opinion of their solidity, Sir James Hunter Blair had been much confirmed by what he had heard and seen in the House of

Commons while he was in parliament, at the time when the laws respecting distilleries were under the consideration of the legislature, and when James Stein got considerable praise for the open and candid manner in which he answered the questions put to him during the investigation of that business. Both James and John Stein, therefore, had been indulged, particularly James, whose business was by far the most extensive, with a degree of credit much beyond the bounds of prudence.

Their transactions, however, were to so large an amount, and our engagement by their drafts running on London, had become so extensive, that, towards the close of the year 1787, I could not help beginning to feel uneasiness at finding ourselves so deeply engaged, that, supposing what was at least possible, they were supporting themselves by a circulation of bills, we were completely in their power; a situation which nothing should ever induce any man of business to allow himself to be brought into by another. The other partners, however, did not view matters in the same alarming light, and appealed to the correctness of Messrs Stein's whole transactions, which, to be sure, was true in every respect, except as to the excessive amount of their London paper, which they had induced us to negotiate for them. Notwithstanding all this, I was resolved to endeavour gradually to reduce the extent of our engagement within more moderate bounds, and we began to take measures to bring this about, although it was a work by no means easy, considering the facilities to which we had accustomed them.

Things were in this situation, when the whole fabric of their credit suddenly fell to the ground by the stoppage of their agents in London, Sandeman and Graham, one of whose acceptances was received with protest by the post of Saturday morning, the February 1788. The necessary consequence was the stoppage also of James Stein and John Stein, and of James and John Haig, distillers at Canonmills near Edinburgh, with whom the Steins had been much connected, and who were embarked in a trade of similar nature.

Besides ourselves, the largest creditors of James Stein were Messrs Allan and Stuart of Edinburgh, who, being extensive dealers in corn, had been induced by their confidence in Messrs Stein's credit to engage in correspondence with them only a very few months preceding, for the purpose of supplying barley for their distillery. As soon as the intelligence arrived from London of Sandeman and Graham's failure, Mr Stuart went over to Killbagie and made an investigation of their affairs, whence it appeared that their engagements were most extensive, particularly those of James Stein, and that there must be a very great loss to their creditors. It appeared also that, for a considerable time, they had been carrying on a losing trade in a foolish and fruitless contest with the London distillers, who, being a great and opulent body of men, had kept down the price of spirits in order to drive their Scotch competitors out of that market—a proof of which was their largely raising the price immediately on those bankruptcies taking place. This contest with the London distillers they had been enabled only to support by their circulation of bills in London, the expenses of which, and the numerous other drawbacks attendant on carrying on a losing trade, had greatly enhanced the mischief.

As there had been a run on our house, by reason of the report that we were largely concerned in the failure of Messrs Fall, although it was well known that we ran the risk of very little ultimate loss by their failure, we had now solid grounds for apprehending a more serious shock to our credit, when it should be known that we were so deeply involved with the Steins, and that they would pay but a very small dividend. Rumour, no doubt, greatly magnifies every circumstance of that nature. Knowing that we had large resources at our command, we had nothing left for us but to face the storm, which we had every reason to expect would take place. As the support of the credit of a banking company, where there is a conviction of safety, is in fact a matter of general concern, the Royal Bank sent us a message by a particular friend at that time in the direction, to let us know that they would receive any bills on London we might have to negotiate, or any paper we might wish to convert into money; and of this friendly offer we so far availed ourselves as to draw for a considerable sum on our bankers in London by way of precaution, in case the demands on us should run higher than we might otherwise conveniently provide for. We also ordered our bankers in London to dispose of as much Bank of England stock and other government securities as would replace the large sum of bills drawn by James and John Stein, and James and John Haig on their agents in London, which had become useless by their failure.

But if the run on the house at the time of the failure of Messrs Fall had been altogether unlooked for, and much more severe than could have been expected, the demands on the house, which took place on the present occasion, were by a great deal more inconsiderable than I had laid my account with. As in the former instance, too, it was chiefly confined, with not above two or three exceptions, to the lower class of depositors, and in three or four days it entirely ceased. This was, no doubt, very much owing to the promptitude with which we satisfied every call that was made on us, and the funds with which we were seen to be prepared to meet the demands that from time to time appeared. On the other hand, we received the most flattering instances of attachment from a numerous body of friends, who, overlooking the imprudence we had been guilty of in going such unwarrantable lengths with those merchants, sought only to know how they could be serviceable to us at such a crisis. Nor did our general business suffer any diminution, so that we had the utmost reason to be thankful to Providence that this misfortune, which at first seemed to threaten our very existence, was finally productive of no other bad consequence to us than the loss of so much money—a loss which I hope will be amply compensated by the lesson of caution it has taught us.

Just before this event took place, the Messrs Hay and I, considering how our numbers, as well as our executive powers, were diminished by the loss of two such valuable and active associates as Sir James Blair and Mr Bartlet, had resolved on the assumption of a new partner; but the difficulty was where to find one endowed with the qualities necessary for our purpose; one possessing knowledge of business, with judgment, application, and good temper, whose character should be so well established in the world as to give us the prospect of going on comfortably and harmoniously together hereafter, as we had been fortunate enough to do hitherto.

After revolving for a considerable time in my mind a subject to us so momentous, and consulting with my friend Mr Farquharson, the accountant, to whose counsel I had been long accustomed to resort on every emergency, I fixed on Mr Samuel Anderson, merchant in Edinburgh, as a gentleman who appeared to be well suited for us. My personal knowledge of Mr Anderson was but slight, and was chiefly founded on the general good character he bore in the world. But Mr John Hay was perfectly well acquainted with his temper and disposition, from having been his school-fellow, and ever since his intimate friend and companion. He therefore gave his warmest approbation of the measure, and a treaty was actually begun with Mr Anderson before Stein's failure, which that event naturally suspended for a little; but as soon as the storm had blown over, and the tranquillity of the house was restored, we resumed the negotiation; and we found no difficulty in satisfying Mr Anderson, by laying before him a statement, shewing both the solidity of our house and the profitable nature of the concern in which we invited him to take a share. He felt no reluctance to join us, and a contract was accordingly drawn up, and executed on the 14th of April 1788, by which Mr Anderson was assumed a partner for the same share which Mr Bartlet had held—a measure with which we have all had much reason to be satisfied, by the harmony that has so uniformly subsisted among us, and the very great assistance we have derived from him in the management of the business.* By his marriage a few years thereafter, he became brother-in-law both to Mr Hay and me, so that we are now linked together by affinity, as well as friendship and mutual interest, in a manner the most comfortable that can be possibly imagined; and our affairs have continued to prosper, by the blessing of Providence on our honest endeavours to discharge our duty to all, greatly beyond our most sanguine expectations.

In the end of this year, 1788, my eldest son, William, returned home; and as I had always destined him for a man of business, with the hope of his one day proving himself worthy of being admitted a partner, he instantly came into the counting-house, and commenced his apprenticeship for the usual period of five years.

Meanwhile everything continued to go on to our utmost wish. Our business gradually increased, as will be seen by the statement in the Appendix, and our sole care was to cultivate the good-will of our employers, not by servility or meanness, but by attention, and a careful and exact discharge of our duty. The arrangement by which Sir John Hunter Blair had, though under age, been admitted a partner, in conformity with my letter to his father, related solely to him; but we now agreed that it should be applied

---

* As, by the terms of the previous contract, it was stipulated that the share of a partner deceasing was to continue till the 31st December subsequent to his death, whereby Mr Bartlet's heirs were entitled to a share of the profits of that year, Mr Anderson would not accept of any share or profit till the year following; yet he instantly began, notwithstanding, to take his share of trouble and responsibility with the rest—a mark of disinterestedness which I feel a pleasure in recording.

[Another instance of the disinterestedness of Mr Anderson may be stated on the authority of an esteemed citizen of Edinburgh, many years deceased. He had been a school-fellow of Henry Dundas, Lord Melville, who, as is well known, had for many years nearly the whole government patronage of Scotland in his hands. His lordship, on a visit to Edinburgh, renewed acquaintance with Mr Anderson, came to dine with him, was introduced to a noble series of sons just entered on manhood, and spent a most cordial and happy evening. He afterwards stated to a friend—and the set of sons makes the remark the more important—that this was the only similar occasion he could recollect when he had not been asked a favour.]

equally to us all, and we therefore entered into an agreement on the 11th March 1789, by which we bound ourselves that, in the event of the death of any of the partners, his eldest son should retain the right to one-third of his father's share, to be held on his account by the surviving partners, but without his having any title to interfere in the management of the business, and with a liberty, at the same time, to him or his guardians, to retire from the concern if he pleased.

In the autumn of this year, 1789, Sir John Hunter Blair returned from Paris, as it was the earnest wish of his mother and all his friends that he should apply heartily to business, not only for his own sake, but that of his numerous younger brothers. Immediately on his arrival, he came into the counting-house for the purpose of mastering details, so as to be fitted for becoming an active partner; and he shewed at first every inclination to fulfil the wishes of his friends; but it was not long before it became obvious that he was by no means qualified for business. He continued, however, to attend the counting-house with more or less interruption till the year 1792, when he left it entirely. By this time the memorable French Revolution had taken place, and hostilities had commenced on the continent, by the irruption into France of the army of Prussians and emigrants under the command of the Duke of Brunswick, in autumn 1792. Still, however, Great Britain had remained quiet, shewing every disposition to continue in peace, and at no period did the prosperity of the country appear to be at a higher pitch. Merchants and manufacturers of every sort had greatly extended their trade, and the public funds had not been so high for many years; but the famous retreat of the Duke of Brunswick's army, and the subsequent successes of the French in Flanders, had so elated the then ruling powers of France, that they meditated the overthrow of every old established government in Europe, and in particular that of Great Britain.

In the prosecution of this design, it was not difficult to find in every state factious and discontented spirits ready to hatch any mischief that might spread confusion, and, if possible, bring about a change of government. Such were by no means wanting either in England or Scotland, and the consequences are well known, that, in order to provide for the safety of the state, government judged it expedient to call out the militia and to summon parliament to meet in the month of December 1792. These proceedings, which obviously foreboded a risk of hostilities, were the signal for a check on mercantile credit all over the kingdom; and that check led, by consequence, to a demand on bankers for the money deposited with them, in order to supply the wants of mercantile men, who, finding an almost total stagnation of trade, were unable to dispose of the goods with which their warehouses were full, or to raise money on them for the payment of running engagements. Numerous bankruptcies in London, and the other great mercantile towns of England, among men who had embarked too deeply in trade and manufactures, were the consequence.

To all this was added another cause of the great and increasing demands on banks—namely, the machinations of the seditious and the apprehensions of the timid. The first wishing to give a blow to the existing government by ruining the credit of the nation, and of all monied people, thereby worked on the fears of the others, so as to create a general alarm and apprehension. This check to circulation, and the consequent demands for money, began to be felt by us, as well as by our neighbours, very early in the year 1793, and rose to such an alarming height as put the demands on the house, that took place in the year 1788, totally out of remembrance. The demand for money at Glasgow, in particular, was uncommonly great, and besides obliging many of the most opulent houses there, in the mercantile and manufacturing line, fairly to acknowledge that they could not fulfil their engagements, it produced the failure of the bank of Murdoch, Robertson, & Co., known by the name of the 'Glasgow Arms Bank,' from the ornament on the top of their circulating notes, and which was one of the three old established banks of that city, although their business had much declined. This happened on the 14th March 1793; and on the 21st of that month, to the very great surprise of everybody, James Dunlop of Glasgow, who was supposed to be one of the most opulent and cautious men of business in the west, was compelled to declare himself bankrupt.* On the 23d April the house of Bertram, Gardner, & Co. of Edinburgh also stopped

* Mr Dunlop had embarked deeply in two branches which, had peace continued and money been plenty, must have made his fortune. Impressed with an idea of the increasing value of land, he had purchased several extensive estates; and having largely engaged in the working of coal-mines, in which he was supposed to be uncommonly skilful, he had reduced these two branches of trade, if so they may be called, to a system by which he proposed every year to accumulate such a sinking fund as should enable him soon to pay off the great debt he was obliged to contract for them, and then leave him in possession of a clear solid landed property; but the war and the consequent scarcity of money disconcerted all his measures, and compelled him to stop payment; the consequence of which was, that his large landed estates being brought to sale at a period when the value had fallen by reason of the pressure of the times, they went at a great depreciation, and his creditors were heavy losers. The same estates, if to be now sold, would fetch far greater prices.

payment, and, to complete the confusion, the four banks of Newcastle, which were known to be opulent, were forced to shut up on the 12th April, owing to their not having had the precaution to keep in readiness sufficient funds to meet the demands that were made upon them. Their stoppage was accompanied by that of a great many country banks in various parts of England, where the trade of banking had been carried to an unwarrantable extent by persons who had not a sufficient foundation, and who, by consequence, were unable to stand the run that the scarcity of money brought upon them. During the whole of this irksome period, I was in Italy, altogether unconscious of what was going on at home, and my partners had been unwilling to alarm me, or to say anything that might induce me to return before the object of our journey—which was the re-establishment of Lady Forbes's health—should be effected. At last, however, things became so serious, and assumed so very alarming an aspect, that they wrote, earnestly requesting me to come home. So little notion had I of anything having happened to require my presence in Scotland, that we were even thinking of spending the summer in Switzerland, and of returning to pass the ensuing winter at Naples. All my letters had brought us accounts that everything was going on smoothly in the counting-house. An interval of a fortnight had taken place, however, without the arrival of any mails from Britain, till the 26th April, when I received a letter from Mr Hay, which astonished me more, I believe, than any I ever received in all my life. It was dated the 30th March, and referred me to one written the preceding post by Mr Anderson, but which I had not then received, as the arrival of the mails was rather irregular. Mr Hay, in his letter, lamented the numerous failures that had taken place, and the consequent run on every bank and banking company, of all which he spoke as supposing me to be perfectly well acquainted, from Mr Anderson's letter, with everything that was passing; and he concluded by saying that, since Mr Anderson had written, there had been a meeting of James Dunlop's creditors, when it appeared there would be a very great deficiency, although he still hoped our loss would not be more than Mr Anderson had called it in his letter, but without specifying what that was. Finally, he concluded by requesting me most earnestly to let no consideration, except Lady Forbes's health, prevent me from coming home without delay. It is scarcely possible to conceive greater astonishment than mine on the perusal of this letter. Numerous bankruptcies I could suppose to have happened in times such as Mr Hay described them to be; but had I been desired to specify the man who, in my opinion, was least likely to become bankrupt, I verily believe I should have named Mr Dunlop, whom I had always considered to be one of the most thriving men in Scotland, as well as one of the most intelligent and active, besides being sober, and economical in his family, and addicted to no unusual personal expense.*

Immediately on receiving Mr Hay's letter—Mr Anderson's did not reach me till the mail following—I at once abandoned all thoughts of remaining longer in Italy. My only consideration was in what manner I could get soonest and best home; but as Lady Forbes was still in a poor state of health, I very much wished her to remain, with our daughter, at Rome, where we had several English friends. She was extremely averse to the idea of being left behind, and wished at least to try how she could bear the journey as far as Florence; that, if when there she found it too much for her, she might remain with an Irish family of our acquaintance, and I could proceed to Scotland by myself.

It was, however, the 8th of May before we were able to begin our journey from Rome. As we were stepping into the carriage, I received a few lines from Mr Hay, dated 13th April, informing me that they had just received information of the four Newcastle banks having been obliged to shut their doors and suspend payments. Knowing the opulence of the partners of these banks, I could not but dread that if the panic had continued to extend itself as far as Edinburgh, our own house might perhaps be at that moment in the same predicament. I had the satisfaction of knowing by the English newspapers that an association had been formed in London, of Northumberland gentlemen, for the purpose of supporting the credit of the Newcastle banks, in consequence of which they had again begun to do business: and next morning I received letters from my partners to let me know that they were going on with credit and respectability, notwithstanding that the demand on them for money still continued exceedingly great. What the final issue might be, however, I could not possibly divine, and I knew that I could not again hear from home for at least three weeks—namely, till we should arrive at Brussels. With all expedition, therefore, we continued our journey, and arrived at Brussels on the 4th of June. On

---

* Mr Dunlop detailed to me all his plans and projects in a very well written letter, which I received from him on my way home, and in which he apologised for having drawn some bills on us just the day before he stopped payment. He said he had done so in an agony of mind not to be described, but that in the uncertainty of his situation, he still flattered himself that, on seeing his friend Mr Gammell from Greenock next day, he might have found it possible to go on.

going to the banker's, I found a packet of letters from Mr Hay. As my former letter from him, which I had received at Florence, was dated 20th April, there was a terrible interval, the events of which I had now to learn, and, considering the gloomy strain of the former, it will not be surprising that I felt a few moments' hesitation before I could break the seal of that which I now received, lest it should have brought tidings of a disastrous nature. To my unspeakable relief, the accounts were highly favourable. Mr Hay informed me that, after his last letter, things had become still worse by the failure of Bertram, Gardner, & Co., which was the signal for a more general and extensive alarm, and the demand for money had been immense, not only on our house, but on Messrs Mansfield & Co. and the Royal Bank, of which he gave me the most convincing proof by enclosing a slip of paper containing the sums we had paid away in the course of one week,* to an amount I should scarcely have thought possible. But he told me likewise not only of the promptitude with which they had been able to make their own payments, but of the help they had been able to afford to other houses who had been put to a nonplus, and who, without our aid, there was great reason to fear, would have been forced to stop, whereby the evil would have been still further increased. Thus we had been able to weather the storm, not only with safety, but with a considerable increase of credit and reputation. And it is impossible for me to do justice to the ability and firmness which my partners had displayed while thus surrounded by the most alarming danger. The exertions they had made to collect our funds and provide against every emergency, were beyond all praise. By the time we arrived in Edinburgh, which was on the 16th June, tranquillity was completely restored, and

* The number of interest-receipts paid from 23d April to 30th April
   inclusive was 603
  The number granted was   60

  More paid than granted, ... 543

In ordinary times the numbers paid and granted are pretty much the same:
  Amount paid above granted in December 1792, . £10,670
  "   "   "   January 1793, .   16,916
  "   "   "   February "   11,561
  "   "   "   March   "   52,961
  "   "   "   April   "   105,075
  "   "   "   to 23d May "   66,541

  Total paid more than granted from Dec. 1792 to 23d May 1793, £263,724

The diminution on account-current balances was in proportion; that is, nearly as much more.

business again flowing in its accustomed channel; also the money which had been drawn out of our hands in the course of the spring soon began again to return, till at last the sum of our deposits far exceeded that of any former period, partly no doubt from the increasing wealth of the country, and partly—perhaps we may be allowed to say without the imputation of vanity—from the regularity and attention with which we have conducted our business, and the desire we have always shewn to accommodate our correspondents as far as prudence warranted.

At the commencement of the following year, 1794, my son William having finished his apprenticeship, and evinced a disposition to become an active man of business, Mr Hay and Mr Anderson were pleased to gratify my wishes by admitting him a partner from that date. In order to do this, we made the following distribution of the $10\frac{2}{3}$ shares which had remained undivided of Sir James Blair's stock, and over which we had retained the power of disposal: Sir W. Forbes, 4; Mr J. Hay, 2; Mr Anderson, 2; Mr Forbes, 2; Mr L. Hay, $\frac{2}{3}$; and the deed of agreement was signed 1st April 1795. In this distribution we omitted Sir John Blair altogether, as he had now withdrawn from the counting-house, and given up all thoughts of being a man of business, although he continued to retain his $5\frac{1}{3}$ shares until the termination of the contract.

During all this while, the war in which the nation was engaged with France, continued to rage with unabated fury in different parts of Europe, and with various success. At the same time, in contradiction to the experience of all former wars Great Britain had been engaged in, which had always checked and diminished the trade of the country, such was now the superior power of the British navy, as evinced by our success at sea, that, while the navy and the trade of France had both been greatly reduced, the commerce of the whole world seemed to centre in this country. France, therefore, strained every nerve to cripple us, and she particularly directed her attention to Ireland, as the most vulnerable part of the British dominions in Europe.

In prosecution of this plan, a formidable squadron with troops on board sailed in a fog from Brest, having thus escaped the vigilance of the British fleet by which that harbour was blockaded, and arrived in Bantry Bay, on the south-west coast of Ireland, in the end of December 1796. Being, however, providentially hindered from landing by tempestuous weather, and not succeeding in their attempt to raise an immediate insurrection in the country, they were obliged to turn and make the best of their way home. Formidable threatenings were also spread abroad on the part of France, of their intention to make a descent on England, which had the effect of creating such an alarm in London, and, indeed, over the country, that the demand for gold on the Bank of England was beyond all former example. Nor was the alarm confined to England. It very soon reached Scotland, and a run on the banks and banking-houses in Edinburgh, similar to that of the year 1793, took place, although fortunately it was but of short duration. It apparently had its commencement from a public meeting of the county of Mid-Lothian, called by the Duke of Buccleuch, the lord-lieutenant, on Friday the 17th February 1797, to concert measures for the defence of the country in case an enemy should attempt to land. The resolutions adopted by that meeting being advertised in the Edinburgh newspapers of Saturday, were perused and commented on next day by the farmers and lower classes of people in the villages throughout the country, who, in consequence, became alarmed, and on Monday the 20th they came to our counting-house in considerable numbers, evidently under the impression of terror, calling for payment of their notes that had been lodged at interest. This lasted the whole of that week, and the two first days of the following. Nor was it confined to us alone, for the public banks experienced it in a still greater degree, and we were beginning to think there was to be a similar, perhaps a still severer, demand on us than what had taken place in 1793; when, early in the morning of Wednesday the 1st March, an express arrived from London to the directors of the Bank of Scotland from Thomas Coutts & Co., their correspondents there, informing them that the demand for gold on the Bank of England had risen to such an alarming height, that the directors had thought it proper to state the circumstance to the Chancellor of the Exchequer, who immediately procured an order of the Privy Council to be issued, prohibiting that bank from making any more issues of specie in exchange for their notes. Mr Mansfield, who was a director of the Bank of Scotland, informed our Mr Anderson of this interesting event, and he immediately brought the intelligence to me, a little before the usual hour of commencing business. My ideas, at various times during the course of the war, had been often not a little gloomy when I thought of the state of things in the kingdom, and indeed in Europe; but now it was that I certainly did think the nation was ruined beyond redemption, when so novel and alarming a circumstance had taken place at the Bank of England, which had ever been considered as the bulwark of public and private credit.

Mr Hay, Mr Anderson, my son, and I, all repaired as fast as possible to the counting-house, which at ten o'clock was crowded as usual with people demanding gold. We were soon joined by Mr Simpson, cashier, by Mr James, deputy-governor of the Royal Bank, and by Mr Fraser, the treasurer of the Bank of Scotland, and we sent for Mr Hog, manager of the British Linen Company, for all ceremony or etiquette of public or private banks was now out of the question, when it had become necessary to think of what was to be done for our joint preservation on such an emergency. Thence we repaired to the Bank of Scotland, where their directors were assembled, and after some time spent in consultation with them, it was agreed that there was no choice left but to follow the example of the Bank of England, and suspend all further payments in specie. The Lord Provost instantly gave orders for calling a meeting of the principal inhabitants that day at two o'clock, which was very numerously attended, considering the shortness of the notice, and amongst others by the Lord President of the Court of Session, the Lord Chief Baron of Exchequer, the Lord Advocate, and the Sheriff of Edinburgh. After stating the order of Council for suspending the payments in specie by the Bank of England, and the similar resolution taken by the banks of Edinburgh, a resolution was instantly and unanimously entered into by those present to give every countenance and support to the Edinburgh banks—including our firm—by receiving their notes in payment with the same readiness as heretofore, and a handbill to that effect was instantly circulated over Edinburgh, and inserted in all the newspapers. Expresses were likewise despatched to Glasgow, Greenock, Paisley, Ayr, Perth, Dundee, and Aberdeen—at all which places there were banks—to inform them of what was passing. The instant this resolution of paying no more specie was known in the street, a scene of confusion and uproar took place, of which it is utterly impossible for those who did not witness it to form an idea.

Our counting-house, and indeed the offices of all the banks, were instantly crowded to the door with people clamorously demanding payment in gold of their interest-receipts, and vociferating for silver in change of our circulating paper. It was in vain that we urged the order of Council—which, however, applied merely to the Bank of England—and the general resolution adopted by all other banks in Edinburgh. They were deaf to every argument, and although no symptom, nor indeed threatening of violence appeared, their noise, and the bustle they made, was intolerable;

which may be readily believed when it is considered that they were mostly of the lowest and most ignorant classes, such as fishwomen, carmen, street-porters, and butchers' men, all bawling out at once for change, and jostling one another in their endeavours who should get nearest to the table, behind which were the cashier and ourselves endeavouring to pacify them as well as we could.

Of our interest-receipts we were prompt in payment; but instead of giving our own circulating notes, as heretofore, we paid the value in notes of the public banks, of which we had an ample supply, and by doing this we were in our own minds satisfied that we fulfilled every obligation, for the sums had been deposited with us, not in specie, but in such notes as we now gave back to the holders. With regard to our circulating notes the case was different. And we felt the hardship on the holders, who were deprived of the means of purchasing with ready money the necessaries of life, as there were no notes of less value than twenty shillings, and it was with the utmost difficulty they could get change anywhere else; for the instant it was known that payments in specie were suspended, not a person would part with a single shilling that they could keep, and the consequence was that both gold and silver specie was hoarded up and instantly disappeared. It was not the want of specie, therefore, that occasioned the distress, but want of confidence, the same as had occasioned the demands on the Bank of England and every other banking society in the kingdom. Saturday was the day on which we had the severest outcry to encounter; for on that day we had always been accustomed to the largest demands for silver to pay wages, and our situation was then really distressing, as many master tradesmen requested in the most earnest manner to have a little silver for enabling them to pay their work-people. All we could do, when sensible that their demand proceeded from *real* necessity, was privately to change a note or two by taking them into a separate room, for we durst not do it openly in the counting-house for fear of raising a riot. In this manner we contrived to keep the people quiet for the first week or so; in the course of which many expedients were thought of; among others, that of issuing tallies of half a crown or five shillings value, which there was every reason to believe would have been highly useful, and most thankfully received by the public. But it was discovered that the doing so was contrary to law, as the act of parliament passed in the year 1764 for correcting the evil of notes for trifling sums, with which the country had been deluged, prohibited the issuing of any substitute for money of less value than twenty shillings.*

At length a partial remedy was found. There chanced to be in London at that time a great quantity of Spanish dollars, worth about four shillings and sixpence each. On these a stamp was affixed at the Mint, by government, which gave them a currency; and as every person issuing notes took care to obtain a supply of these, they answered tolerably well the purpose of change. Quarter guineas, too, were coined at the Mint; and in a short time an act of parliament was passed to permit such banking-companies as had been in the practice of issuing circulating paper, to issue notes of five shillings value during a limited time. Of this permission, the Royal Bank and several country banks availed themselves; and I have no doubt they were considerable profiters by the measure. For as these notes mostly passed into places of the lowest traffic, they soon became so torn and ragged that they would scarcely hang together; and many of them must doubtless have been entirely destroyed, so as never to return for payment on the issuers. We did not issue any notes of that description; being convinced that there was no real scarcity of specie in the country, and that it would again make its appearance when the panic should wear off, as actually proved to be the case.

In two or three months, when confidence seemed to be tolerably well restored, we began again to issue our notes of one pound and upwards as formerly, and they were just as well received as ever; so that our circulation, which had diminished greatly while we ceased to issue, again swelled to its former amount. And it was matter of agreeable surprise to see in how short a time, after the suspension of paying in specie, the run on us ceased. Indeed, when the holders found they could not succeed in obtaining payment in gold, they desisted from demanding the value; appearing to be equally well satisfied to retain our promissory-notes bearing interest, instead of receiving the value in circulating notes of the other banks, which bore no interest, and for which they could no more get specie from them than from us. It was remarkable, also, after the first surprise and alarm was over, how quietly the country submitted, as they still do, to transact all business by means of bank-notes, for which the issuers give no specie as formerly. The wonder was the greater, because the act

* Some people adopted the ingenious method of tearing a twenty-shilling note into halves or quarters, and paying them away accordingly; and when such were presented to us, we always paid the value of the fragment without hesitation.

of the Privy Council first, and afterwards the act of parliament, applied merely, as I have already said, to the Bank of England, while all other banks, both in England and Scotland, were left to carry on their business without any protection from parliament, and without any means of obtaining specie beyond what the natural course of business brought into their hands from the gold circulating in the country. That source, however, has hitherto proved amply sufficient for all needful purposes.*

From this time forward the business of our house went on, not only with the utmost smoothness, but increased, along with that wonderful extension of the commerce and manufactures of the country of which I have already taken notice, and which, contrary to all former example, continued to swell as the war was protracted. In this situation we continued steadily to adhere to the genuine and salutary principles of banking business, by employing our funds on cash-accounts and in discounting bills which we deemed safe, as far as the trade of this part of the country required. Besides the sum employed on these purposes, we made a large deposit in the two senior public banks of Edinburgh, which, although it yielded but a low interest, we yet judged to be a necessary precaution, in order to guard against the effects of any unforeseen emergency. Still further, we invested for the same purpose at London a part of the money deposited with us in Exchequer and Navy Bills, which, yielding an excellent interest, were always an available resource against any unexpected demand, while they were not subject to such accidental depreciations as the other public funds.

It has been a rule with us, from which we have never departed, to avoid everything that might be termed stock-jobbing, and for that reason we never held any share in the loan raised annually by government during the war. There was one species of govern-

---

* The forbearance of the Scottish people, and their confidence in the solidity of their banks, has been such that no attempt has ever been made to enforce payment in specie by legal process. Nor in England did I ever hear of its being tried, except at Bury St Edmund's, where a Mr Grigby, holder of some notes of the bank there of Messrs Oakes and Son, brought an action against them in July 1801 for refusing to pay in specie. But as the bank of Bury St Edmund's had offered to pay him in notes of the Bank of England, which proved that they were sufficiently provided with funds for the purpose, and as it evidently appeared on the trial that the demand for gold was unnecessary, and the action itself proceeded from malevolence, Mr Baron Hotham, the judge before whom the action was brought, severely reprobated the plaintiff's conduct. The point of law was left to be tried by the Court of King's Bench; but I never heard more of it, and probably the question was dropped, on being found to be so unpopular.

ment securities, however, in which we invested some money without scruple, from time to time, and that was in the fund denominated Short Annuities. These had been granted for a term of years for money borrowed by government in the year [1778], and they expire on the 5th January 1808, till which period they are paid regularly every half-year, and this price was so low during the war, that he who purchased them had an absolute certainty of realising a very handsome profit at their termination.

Therefore, finding our money swell upon our hands beyond all that we could employ in the ordinary purposes of our business, and it being absolutely necessary to place the surplus so as to yield us a fair return, as we were paying to our customers a considerable interest, we purchased some of these short annuities from time to time. Another public fund also presented itself, which we considered might be held with safety and advantage. The Chancellor of the Exchequer having resolved to convert a portion of the Navy Bills into stock bearing interest at five per cent., under the stipulation of redeeming it at par, if the holders should demand their money, at the end of two years after the termination of the war; and, as we happened to hold a large sum of Navy Bills, we of course became possessed of a considerable amount of this five per cent. stock. Besides that stock, the holders of Navy Bills received another portion of their value in four per cent. stock irredeemable, but on such low terms, that, seeing no prospect of having occasion to sell it till the return of peace, when, in all probability, it would rise considerably in value, we resolved to take it also, and to keep the whole, as well as some three per cents. which we ventured to purchase at a very low rate. These purchases we did not consider as any departure from our resolution of avoiding speculation in government securities, because we never bought to the value of a shilling without paying for it in money, nor even that, except when we did not know how otherwise to employ our funds, after having discounted every good bill that was offered to us. And we had solid ground for deeming these investments as a source of considerable future profit, when it should please God to send us again the blessing of peace—a profit of the certainty of which nothing could disappoint us, except our being forced to part with the stock in the interval, and of that there was very little probability, so well fortified were we against any demands likely to happen by the amount of our other resources to meet them, without being compelled to break in upon our investment in the funds.

But there was another circumstance relating to these investments which now engaged our attention, and that was the consideration that if any of the partners should die before the return of peace, there would be a degree of hardship if his family were deprived of a share in the expected advantages to arise from them on the war ceasing.

This consideration induced the partners, on the 17th May 1798, to enter into an agreement whereby they prolonged the contract, which would otherwise have expired on the 31st December 1799, to one year after the termination of the war, during which prolonged period, if any of us should die, our interest in the house should continue to our children to the same extent as *their* father had enjoyed, but with a deduction of twenty per cent. from the share of the net profit, as some compensation to the surviving partners for the additional trouble they would be subjected to by being deprived of their colleague's assistance.

On the 31st December 1799, the contract which we had entered into with Sir John Hunter Blair terminated, when, of course, his interest in the house came to an end, and we divided the shares held by him, with the addition of two of mine, which I ceded to my son, in the following manner : namely, Sir W. Forbes, 18 ; Mr John Hay, 11 ; Mr Samuel Anderson, 11 ; Mr Lewis Hay, 4 ; Mr William Forbes, 4—in all, 48 parts.

In no long time after this arrangement, we had the misfortune to lose our worthy friend and partner, Mr Lewis Hay, who, I have strong reason to suspect, fell a martyr to his intense and persevering application to business. He had contracted a severe cold towards the end of February 1800, which, however, did not prevent him from coming up stairs—for his dwelling-house was under the same roof with the counting-house—to transact business as usual, until Friday the 21st, when he did not come up in the afternoon, a thing very uncommon with him. From this time his illness increased, ending in inflammation of the lungs, and he died on Friday the 28th February, leaving a widow and six young children. He had married rather late in life, prevented, doubtless, from thinking of it sooner from the peculiar situation of his affairs.

I have already expressed the high opinion I entertained of Mr Hay's merits. In the whole of his conduct in life he was methodical to a singular degree ; he was most exemplary in his morals, and strict in the discharge of all the duties of external religion, possessed of a high sense of honour, and the most inflexible integrity. He was fond of reading, and was by no means unacquainted with books, particularly those of a serious cast ; and I remember my mother—who was very fond of Mr Hay—used to interchange with him old-fashioned books of divinity,

to which they both seemed partial. Although naturally grave in
his deportment, yet no man more delighted to unbend his mind
at table in the midst of a circle of select friends. But his
prevailing feature was application to business, from which he
never allowed any object whatever to withdraw his attention.* His
death, therefore, was a very great misfortune to us; for, although
he very much left to his partners the general management of the
business of the house, yet we reaped much advantage from his
being constantly over the clerks, as well as from the exactness
with which he filled an essential department. Yet with all this
precision and method in the business of the house, he did not leave
behind him either a statement or a settlement of his own affairs,
nor any nomination of guardians to his young family, so that an
application to the Court of Session became necessary. The court
appointed Mrs Hay, an excellent woman, and one of her relations,
along with three of us, to take care of them and their concerns.
Although he had not been many years in business, yet by the
prosperous state of our house, and his own and Mrs Hay's attention to economy, he left his children sufficiently well provided for.
The death of Sir John Hunter Blair happened in May 1800; he
had always something peculiar and eccentric in his manner, which
gradually increased as he grew older, until at last he became totally
deprived of his reason, from which melancholy state he never
recovered. My partners and I continued desirous that some one
of our late worthy friend, Sir James Blair's sons, should become
interested in our house, of which he had been so conspicuous a
member; and when we perceived that his eldest son would not
apply himself to business, the third son James—for the second son,
David, had by that time succeeded to his mother's estate of
Dunskey—was sent to Hamburgh, and having remained there a
considerable time, he returned to Edinburgh and entered our
counting-house, in order to qualify himself for being admitted a

* I recollect an incident which strongly marked this. When his mother
died, he sent over the key of his desk to the counting-house, along with a
message, to tell us what had happened, and to say that he should be detained
an hour or so later than usual. I went over immediately, and called on him,
and requested that he would not think of coming out until the funeral should
be over; but I found him preparing to come to the counting-house. He was
conscious, he said, of having discharged his duty to his mother while she
lived. He had given the necessary orders in preparation for the funeral, and
therefore he could not think of being absent from his duty to us. To those
who did not know him, this might have appeared a degree of heartless unconcern
on such an occasion; but we, who knew him, considered it in its true light—as
a part of his uniform attention to the discharge of his duty in every station of
life.

partner. The death of his eldest brother, however, having put him in possession of Dunskey—in place of the next brother David (now become Sir David), on the latter succeeding to the family estate—he also gave over thoughts of being a man of business, and withdrew from the counting-house. Still preserving our original wish of having one of the family, if possible, as an associate, Sir James's fifth son, Forbes Hunter Blair—Robert, the fourth, having gone into the army—was sent for from Liverpool, where he had been placed for the purpose of mercantile education, and entered our counting-house, with the view of being one day assumed a partner.*

Feeling, as we did, the loss of Mr Lewis Hay, it became desirable for us to have a steady, useful partner in his place, who should also occupy the residence attached to the counting-house; and we had no hesitation in making choice of Mr Patrick Maxton, who had long been with us, and at that time filled the important office of our first cashier. Mr Maxton had reached the middle period of life, and had given ample proof of his fitness for the trust. On the 11th August 1800, we admitted him as a partner into the house during the continuance of our present contract, and allotted to him the twenty per cent. received on the share of profits belonging to Mr Hay's family, in terms of our agreement of 1798, together with a further allowance, which should secure his having not less than £300 per annum.

At length, on the 1st October 1801, preliminaries of peace were signed, and on the 27th March 1802, a definitive treaty of peace was entered into between Great Britain and France, which ended for a time the most bloody and destructive war that ever was waged in Europe. The period was thus ascertained—namely, the 30th June 1803—at which our contract of copartnery was to terminate, and the interest in it of Mr Lewis Hay's family to cease. On the cessation of the war, the expected rise in the public funds having taken place, we were able to dispose of a considerable part of our stock investments to great advantage. But we retained the short annuities and five per cent. stock, conformably to our original intention, until the one shall expire, and the other come to the period when it is to be paid off at par, two years after the conclusion of the war.

Nothing further occurred in our house of any importance until the year 1803, when our contract being about to terminate, we

* [Mr Forbes Hunter Blair contested the representation of Edinburgh, unsuccessfully, with Mr Jeffrey and Mr Abercrombie, at the first election after the passing of the Reform Act in 1832. He died in 1833.]

have this day—17th May 1803—signed a new one, to commence from the 30th June ensuing, and to last for ten and a half years, namely, until the 31st December 1813, by which the shares of the house are now held as follow: Sir William Forbes, 17; Mr John Hay, 11; Mr Samuel Anderson, 11; Mr William Forbes, 5; Mr Patrick Maxton, 2; Mr Forbes Hunter Blair, 2—in all, 48 shares. The stock of the company, which in the former contract had been stated at £9000, is by the new contract augmented to £24,000, as a security to the public, along with the separate and aggregate property of the partners, which is to no inconsiderable amount.

On this occasion I cannot help remarking the singular vicissitudes of the present times. After the concluding of the Treaty of Amiens, we certainly thought that we should have had an interval of peace for some years; yet in very little more than a twelvemonth, we find the nation again involved in a war with France, of which no human being can foresee the event or the probable termination. Yet let us not despond, but trust that the Almighty Being, who has on many occasions so wonderfully preserved this country, will still continue his protection, and in no long period restore to us the blessings of peace. In the meantime, may we, who are associated together in an important business, continue, by the same harmony among ourselves, and the same unremitting attention and prudence as heretofore, so to conduct the affairs of our house, that, by the blessing of Divine Providence, it may still prosper as it has hitherto done.

Statement of the Business of the Banking-house in Edinburgh formerly under the Firm of Coutts Brothers & Co. and John Coutts & Co., now under the Firm of Sir William Forbes, James Hunter, & Co.

	Amount of the Balances.	Notes Payable.	Bills and Notes Renewable.	Amount of the London Account.	Bills to the Excise.	Gross Profit.	Net Profit.	Bad Debts wrote off.
1st May 1754	£39,832 8 6	£18,054 5 10	£4,654 19 5					
31st Dec.								
1764	58,362 15 1	25,597 9 8	9,931 0 5	£178,731 4 11	£57,600	£2862 9 9½	£2665 9 10	£40 0 0
1765	78,445 5 10	31,510 14 8	15,978 13 8	188,837 15 1	44,800	2620 14 5	2401 12 6	
1766	88,697 2 6	28,468 10 4	18,945 19 7	204,220 6 7	35,500	2713 15 1	2434 8 9	
1767	82,966 10 1	21,694 8 7	10,399 17 2	206,135 15 3	38,550	2418 15 0	2186 8 10	
1768	81,467 2 10	26,279 8 9	9,889 5 4	191,001 10 5	46,200	2960 9 2	2710 8 9	
1769	74,291 13 6	18,433 3 6	3,746 0 10	218,568 19 11	59,100	2673 13 8	2384 4 0	39 15 6
1770	71,578 5 9	19,250 3 6	3,605 1 9	191,287 16 10	56,500	2510 13 4	2207 7 0	273 1 3
1771	90,751 7 7	23,272 13 10	2,582 19 9	224,653 0 1	56,300	2740 5 10	2370 13 4	12 0 0
1772	84,604 19 6	19,020 11 8	4,584 13 1	440,529 18 3	56,600	3570 19 6	2900 3 0	699 8 4
1773	101,787 11 7	22,265 17 10	3,411 15 3	307,745 1 1	47,000	3481 1 6	2955 16 5	1184 15 3
1774	107,154 7 2	34,353 10 5	9,198 12 7	227,314 2 0	35,600	3244 11 1	2563 7 0	26 18 8
1775	128,009 19 2	66,491 0 3	15,473 1 1	276,400 2 7	46,000	2818 1 10	2108 18 8	1943 8 8
1776	181,858 1 10	68,711 17 10	25,615 8 3	292,752 17 11	45,800	3763 7 7	3323 13 3	
1777	194,778 11 6	104,322 8 0	30,854 7 1	302,562 0 8	69,750	4034 12 4	3249 0 11	
1778	143,637 7 4	68,006 1 5	29,347 9 9	276,926 8 9	87,340	3859 6 0	3230 14 6	1229 19 0
1779	171,237 6 6	99,863 5 10	29,071 10 8	286,763 10 6	74,600	3731 5 3	2922 4 11	

*** Since the publication of the first edition, a letter written by Sir William Forbes to his partners, Mr (afterwards Sir) John Hay and Mr Samuel Anderson, has been put into the hands of the Editor, who finds it to involve so exemplary an instance of commercial justice and magnanimity, that he sought permission to place it before the public.

To JOHN HAY and SAMUEL ANDERSON, Esqrs.

'BANTASKINE, *July* 24, 1799.

'DEAR SIRS—I wrote to Mr Hay the 20th, since which I have not had the pleasure of hearing. Knowing how extremely occupied you both are, it is exactly my wish that you should not take the trouble of writing, or bestow the time on it, uselessly, except when there is anything of moment to say.

'Since I came to the country, a thought has occurred to me, which I have been turning in my mind, and which I now wish to state for your consideration. It is, in regard to the prolongation of our contract. The very peculiar circumstances of the times, particularly with respect to our investment in the funds, made it an expedient measure that, in the event of the death of any of the partners, his interest should still continue in the house, notwithstanding the clause in the contract which says it should cease in such an event; as it appeared to be a hardship that the family of a deceasing partner should be subjected to the loss which possibly might ensue, if the price of that investment should be considerably under what the funds were bought at; while, on the other hand, there was reason to hope the price would rise in the event of a peace. To continue the contract, therefore, seemed a wise measure for us all; but it was particularly so to me, who am considerably the oldest of our number. But although it did then, and still does appear to have been proper to do so, with regard to our investment, there seems to be no reason why such an alteration in the respective interests of the partners, with regard to the general profits of the house, should not be made at the 1st January next, as would, in all probability, have taken place if our present contract had been left to expire at that period. For, surely, in framing a new contract, it would have been but equitable that the shares of the house should be more equally divided than they are at present. Twelve years since the contract was last made, have brought us much nearer to an equality than we were at that period; and as the whole load of the business, which you manage with so much care, attention, and ability, may be said to press entirely upon you two, it is no more than common justice that your shares should be augmented, in order that you may have a decent recompense for such uncommon labour. For my own part, for a long time past I have been able to free you of very little of the burthen; and my health renders me now still more incapable to take what used to be my ordinary share of the fatigue and attendance. What I would propose, therefore, would be to fix the shares of each partner, from the 1st January next, in such a manner as they would have been divided had we been framing a new contract to commence at that period. With regard to our investment in the funds, indeed, I shall be extremely glad that our respective interests in it with regard to the ultimate profit or loss, at the period to which we have prolonged the contract, shall continue the same as they are at present. We have borne the brunt of the battle together, and I hope we shall in due time reap the fruits of the victory. But, with regard to the ordinary profits arising from the established and regular business of the house, we may throw these into such a division of shares at the 1st January next, as would have been the case had we been framing a new contract. What that division should be, we can talk of at meeting. I merely state the principle to you at present, in order that you may be reflecting on it, and considering in what way the shares should be distributed. Those held at present by Sir J. Blair will, of course, fall in to us when the contract expires; and such a proportion may be left undisposed of, as was done on a former occasion, as it may be thought right to reserve for his brother, if, on a sufficient trial, we shall judge him proper to be assumed as a partner at some future period. I once thought, and indeed it was what seemed to occur to us all, at the time of prolonging the present contract, that the respective shares might continue as they are at present till the end of the war; but, as that is yet a distant and still very uncertain period, although it is the best possible for winding up our investment, if it please God to continue to prosper us so as that we can hold it till then; yet there is no reason why the ordinary profits which, in so great a degree, arise from your labour and exertions, should not be more equally divided in the meantime than they are at present. I am most grateful to Heaven that we have been so fortunate hitherto in the prosecution of our business, and the uninterrupted harmony that has subsisted among us, I consider as one of the greatest blessings of my life; and, therefore, I feel the stronger call on me to propose to do you the justice to which you are so fairly entitled. That the same good-fortune, and the same harmony may ever attend us, is the sincere prayer of, my dear friends,

Your most affectionate Bro^r, and very humble Servt,

WILLIAM FORBES.

JOHN HAY and SAMUEL ANDERSON, Esq^{rs}.'

Edinburgh:
Printed by W. and R. Chambers.

www.ingramcontent.com/pod-product-compliance
Lightning Source LLC
Chambersburg PA
CBHW022148160426
43197CB00009B/1471